Proceedings of the
19th International Congress of Classical Archaeology

Volume 46: Town-Country Relations in the Northern Parts of *Germania inferior* from an Economic Perspective

Proceedings of the
19th International Congress of Classical Archaeology

Cologne/Bonn, 22 – 26 May 2018
Archaeology and Economy in the Ancient World

Edited by

Martin Bentz and Michael Heinzelmann

Volume 46

ICCA XIX AIAC

Edited by

Marion Brüggler – Julia Obladen-Kauder – Harry van Enckevort

Town-Country Relations in the Northern Parts of *Germania inferior* from an Economic Perspective

Panel 8.9

Propylaeum
SPECIALIZED INFORMATION SERVICE CLASSICS

Bibliographic information published by the Deutsche Nationalbibliothek:
The Deutsche Nationalbibliothek lists this publication in the Deutsche Nationalbibliografie;
detailed bibliographic data are available on the Internet at http://dnb.dnb.de.

Propylaeum
SPECIALIZED INFORMATION SERVICE CLASSICS

Published at Propylaeum,
Heidelberg University Library 2020.

This publication is freely available under https://www.propylaeum.de (Open Access).
URN: urn:nbn:de:bsz:16-propylaeum-ebook-727-7
DOI: https://doi.org/10.11588/propylaeum.727

Editorial Coordination: Florian Birkner, Ina Borkenstein, Christian Schöne
Editorial Staff: Stefanie Herten, Katharina Zerzeropulos

Layout: Torsten Zimmer, Zwiebelfisch@quarium

Cover illustration: Cows coming home after a day of grazing in the flood basin of the Biebzra (Poland) in 1995. The scene could have taken place in Roman times on the Lower Rhine. Photo: L. I. Kooistra

ISBN: 978-3-948465-87-2
e-ISBN: 978-3-948465-86-5

Universität zu Köln

UNIVERSITÄT BONN

CONTENTS

PREFACE

On behalf of the 'Associazione Internazionale di Archaeologica Classica (AIAC)' the 19th International Congress for Classical Archaeology took place in Cologne and Bonn from 22 to 26 May 2018. It was jointly organized by the two Archaeological Institutes of the Universities of Cologne and Bonn, and the primary theme of the congress was 'Archaeology and Economy in the Ancient World'. In fact, economic aspects permeate all areas of public and private life in ancient societies, whether in urban development, religion, art, housing, or in death.

Research on ancient economies has long played a significant role in ancient history. Increasingly in the last decades, awareness has grown in archaeology that the material culture of ancient societies offers excellent opportunities for studying the structure, performance, and dynamics of ancient economic systems and economic processes. Therefore, the main objective of this congress was to understand economy as a central element of classical societies and to analyze its interaction with ecological, political, social, religious, and cultural factors. The theme of the congress was addressed to all disciplines that deal with the Greco-Roman civilization and their neighbouring cultures from the Aegean Bronze Age to the end of Late Antiquity.

The participation of more than 1.200 scholars from more than 40 countries demonstrates the great response to the topic of the congress. Altogether, more than 900 papers in 128 panels were presented, as were more than 110 posters. The publication of the congress is in two stages: larger panels are initially presented as independent volumes, such as this publication. Finally, at the end of the editing process, all contributions will be published in a joint conference volume.

We would like to take this opportunity to thank all participants and helpers of the congress who made it such a great success. Its realization would not have been possible without the generous support of many institutions, whom we would like to thank once again: the Universities of Bonn and Cologne, the Archaeological Society of Cologne, the Archaeology Foundation of Cologne, the Gerda Henkel Foundation, the Fritz Thyssen Foundation, the Sal. Oppenheim Foundation, the German Research Foundation (DFG), the German Academic Exchange Service (DAAD), the Romano-Germanic Museum Cologne and the LVR-LandesMuseum Bonn. Finally, our thanks go to all colleagues and panel organizers who were involved in the editing and printing process.

Bonn/Cologne, in August 2019

Martin Bentz & Michael Heinzelmann

Vergleichende Ergebnisse der Beziehungen zwischen Stadt und Land der *civitas Batavorum* (mit Oppidum, *Ulpia Noviomagus* und Militärstandort) sowie der *civitas Cugernorum* (mit vorcoloniazeitlicher Siedlung und *Colonia Ulpia Traiana*): Siedlungsstrukturen, Landwirtschaft und Ernährung

Julia Obladen-Kauder

In der folgenden Sektion werden zwei benachbarte *civitates* der Germania inferior in Bezug auf ihre ökonomischen Stadt-Land-Beziehungen einander gegenübergestellt. Es handelt sich um die *civitas Batavorum* und die *civitas Cugernorum* mit ihren jeweiligen Hauptorten Nijmegen und Xanten. Einleitend ist festzustellen, dass es in einigen Bereichen zum Teil gravierende Defizite gibt, die entweder forschungsgeschichtlich bedingt sind oder aber auf naturgegebenen Befundsituationen beruhen.

So werden in der *civitas Batavorum* rund 1000 ländliche Siedlungen angenommen, von denen viele archäologisch untersucht sind. Im Raum Xanten sind bislang nur zehn ländliche Siedlungen ausgegraben worden, so dass sich Vergleiche (noch) nicht haltbar ziehen lassen. Dies wird sich in den nächsten Jahren bzw. Jahrzehnten durch die inzwischen programmatisch aufgelegten Konzepte des LVR-Amtes für Bodendenkmalpflege im Rheinland zu archäologischen Untersuchungen in großen Kiesabbaugebieten hoffentlich erfolgreich verändern.

Sowohl die archäobotanischen Proben aus Befunden der römischen Zivilsiedlung Nijmegens als auch die Tierknochen aus der *Colonia Ulpia Traiana* wurden noch nicht (vollständig) untersucht (z. B. Strontium-Isotopie) bzw. noch nicht hinreichend publiziert. Aussagen zu agrarischen Produkten stammen in Nijmegen überwiegend aus militärischem Kontext. Knochen im Bereich der ländlichen Siedlungen der *civitas Cugernorum* haben sich aufgrund der Bodenbeschaffenheit nicht erhalten, sodass wir hier nur indirekte Hinweise auf Viehhaltung durch die Bauweise der Häuser und durch vereinzelte Viehglöckchen im archäologischen Fundgut haben. Mangels zeitgenössischer Ausgrabungen bzw. wegen des Fehlens von Bodenproben aus den alten Untersuchungen in militärischen Bereichen des Xantener Raumes sind Aussagen zu archäobotanischem Material so gut wie nicht vorhanden.

Naturgemäß sind in beiden Städten sowie in den Villen und Tempeln der *civitas Batavorum* die steinernen Baumaterialien ausnahmslos importiert, so zum Beispiel Grauwacke, Kalkstein und Tuff aus dem Mosel-, Rhein- und Eifelraum sowie Marmor aus dem Mittelmeerraum. Für die *Colonia Ulpia Traiana* gibt es außerdem den Nachweis von Bauhölzern aus dem Odenwald und dem Schwarzwald. Bei den ländlichen Siedlungen handelte es sich in beiden *civitates* in der Regel um Einzelhöfe und kleine

Weiler nach traditionellem vorrömischen Muster. Im Unterschied zu Xanten gibt es jedoch im Hinterland von Nijmegen auch Nachweise über römische Villen. Dort sind Importe von Ziegeln aus De Holdeurn belegt.

Hinsichtlich der Versorgung der römischen Zivilsiedlungen bzw. Städte mit ackerbaulichen Produkten, insbesondere Weizenarten für die Brotherstellung, ergibt sich für Nijmegen zumindest eine teilweise Versorgung aus dem Umland. In Xanten hingegen haben wir unerklärlicherweise dafür bislang keinen Nachweis, obwohl 70% der Böden von ausreichend guter Qualität sind für den Anbau von Feldfrüchten (davon hätten immerhin 27% eine Qualität, die Dinkelanbau zuließe) und eine Überschussproduktion möglich gewesen wäre. Vielleicht war die Stadtbevölkerung der *Colonia Ulpia Traiana* ja einfach nur „verwöhnt" und bevorzugte qualitativ hochwertige Ackerbauprodukte aus der fruchtbaren Lößbörde des südlichen Rheinlands bzw. aus noch weiter entfernt liegenden Regionen. Wahrscheinlich handelt es sich aber auch nur um einen momentanen Forschungsstand. Als fassbare Strategie, wie der Lebensmittelfluss vom Land in die Stadt funktioniert hat, wird für den Bereich der *civitas Batavorum* angenommen, dass es zentrale Sammelstandorte gab, von denen aus die Verteilung stattfand.

Überregionale Importe von luxuriösen Nahrungsmitteln und Baumaterialien, zum Teil aus dem Mittelmeerraum, lassen sich in beiden Zentralorten nachweisen. Weitgehend noch unklar ist hingegen, was der Landbevölkerung auf den Märkten in der *Ulpia Noviomagus* und *Colonia Ulpia Traiana* an eigenen städtischen Produkten zum Verkauf angeboten wurde. Für Xanten wird angenommen, dass es zwar recht viele unterschiedliche Gewerbebetriebe in der vorcoloniazeitlichen Siedlung gab, die Erzeugnisse aber kaum in der Region abgesetzt worden sind. Für das 2./3. Jahrhundert wird aufgrund der bisherigen Forschungsergebnisse gar eine Abnahme der Produktion für möglich gehalten. Insgesamt sind hier weitere Untersuchungen in Siedlungen des Umlandes hinsichtlich römischen Fundgutes abzuwarten.

Es war nicht Gegenstand der Betrachtungen, ob auch die rechtsrheinischen Gebiete hinsichtlich der Versorgung der Städte mit Nahrungsmitteln einbezogen werden sollen oder müssen. Immerhin gibt es auch dort römische Funde im ländlichen Raum, die wechselseitige Beziehungen wahrscheinlich machen.

Abschließend wurde angeregt, dass auf deutscher Seite eine deutliche Intensivierung der Forschungen im Hinterland stattfinden muss, um die Parameter vergleichbar(er) zu machen. Dabei ist der Focus auch wesentlich auf den Einsatz naturwissenschaftlicher Untersuchungen zur Herkunftsbestimmung von agrarischen Produkten zu richten. Des Weiteren müssen die Ergebnisse als Grundlage weiterer Diskussionen zeitnah veröffentlicht werden.

	Nijmegen: Oppidum, *Ulpia Noviomagus* und Legionslager	**Umland/Hinterland (ländliche Siedlungen & „Villenlandschaft“)**	**Xanten: vorcoloniazeitliche Siedlung & *Colonia Ulpia Traiana***	**Umland/Hinterland (ländliche Siedlungen)**
Bedeutung/ Einordnung	Zentralort der *civitas Batavorum*		Zentraler Marktort der *civitas Cugernorum*; Handel mit agrarischen Produkten (Überschuss) aus dem Umland; Erwerb wichtiger „städtischer“ Produkte (Küchengeschirr, Werkzeuge u.a.m.) durch die Landbevölkerung	
Bevölkerungszahl militärisch & zivil	fünfstellig (rd. 10.000)		fünfstellig (>/= 10.000)	
landwirtschaftlich geprägte Siedlungen		rd. 1000 (geschätzt)		10 (archäologisch untersucht)
Lage der Siedlungen		Lage der batavischen *civitas* im 2. Jh. in einer Pufferzone zwischen den reichen gallischen Provinzen und den germanischen Stämmen nördlich des Rheins		Donken und saale-eiszeitliche Endmoräne (keine Besiedlung von feuchten und sumpfigen Gebieten!); kaum Erkenntnisse in der Rheinaue wegen der starken nachrömischen Überprägung durch die Flussbettverlagerungen
Siedlungs-strukturen		Ländliche Siedlungen: kleine Bauerngemeinschaften mit eigener batavischer (vorgeschichtlicher) Identität und Traditionen, z.B. Bauweise; „Villenlandschaft“: Villen kommen vorwiegend rund um Nijmegen vor		Einzelhöfe mit Häusern in traditioneller Holz-Lehmbauweise; Hausaufteilung in den ländlichen Siedlungen mit Wohn-Stallteil lässt auf Viehzucht schließen
Baumaterialien	Einheimische Ziegelproduktion in De Holdeurn (**legio X**: 71–105 n. Chr.)	„Villenlandschaft“ und Tempel: Dachziegel aus De Holdeurn, Fundamente mit importierter Grauwacke (Bauweise in gallo-romanischer Tradition)	Einheimische Produktion in der Xantener Legionsziegelei	Bereits in der Eisenzeit existieren keine ausgedehnten Wälder mehr, d.h. Bauholz ist regional knapp (Entwicklung von Heidelandschaften).

Tabelle 1: Die Ergebnisse im Vergleich. Auswertung der Beiträge und der Diskussion nach dem Vortragsblock am 25. Mai 2018.

	Nijmegen	Umland/Hinterland	Xanten	Umland/Hinterland
Ackerbau	Daten hauptsächlich aus dem militärischen Bereich, Proben aus Ulpia Noviomagus noch nicht ausgewertet; Gemüse, Früchte und Nüsse stammen aus Gärten innerhalb der Stadt; 70% der Ernährung der Stadtbevölkerung besteht aus Getreide; hypothetische Bedarfsberechnung bei 10.000 Menschen: $1.2x10^6$ kg Getreide im Jahr; 50% des benötigten Getreides (nur Emmer und „non-bread-cereals") stammen aus dem Umland, außerdem auch noch Gerste, Hirse und Hafer; Dinkel wurde importiert, vielleicht aus den fruchtbaren Lößgebieten des südlichen Rheinlands; außerdem ggf. auch noch Feldfrüchte, z. B. Linse und Erbse	Auf Uferwallbereichen, knapp über Flusshöhe; Nutzung fruchtbarer Böden mit Flussablagerungen; aus dem Vergleich zwischen 35 ländlichen Siedlungen mit der Stadt Nijmegen: Anbau von Emmer zur Brotherstellung für die Stadtbevölkerung; daneben Gerste, Hirse und Hafer; bei Hülsenfrüchten, Gemüse und Kräuter unklar, ob Anbau nur für den Eigenbedarf oder auch für die Stadtbevölkerung; zentral gelegene Getreidespeicher, von denen aus die Verteilung organisiert wurde; Überschussproduktion von Getreide (Emmer, Gerste, Hirse und Hafer) im ländlichen Raum: $7.5x10^6$ (=7.500.000) kg/Jahr, mehr als ausreichend für die Ernährung der Stadtbewohner und die Landbevölkerung.	Bislang keinen nennenswerten Übereinstimmungen der hochwertigen Getreidearten, wie Dinkel zwischen CUT und den ländlichen Siedlungen, keine Versorgung mit Brotweizensorten aus dem unmittelbaren Umland sondern aus weiter entfernten Gebieten mit besserer Bodenqualität, z.B. Lößgebiete im südlichen Rheinland	Überschwemmungsfreie, leicht erhöhte Bereiche; „non-villa-landscape" mit lehmig-sandigen Böden; rund 70% der Böden sind jedoch tauglich für den Anbau von Feldfrüchten, davon immerhin 27% für Dinkel und 42% für Gerste; die ländlichen Siedlungen halten an der eisenzeitlichen Ackerbautradition fest; obwohl die Voraussetzungen für eine Überschussproduktion im Ackerbau gegeben waren, wurde die CUT offensichtlich nicht mit hochwertigen Getreidesorten, wie Dinkel aus dem Hinterland versorgt.
Viehzucht	Größter Anteil an Rind (älteres Schlachtalter als im Umland) im städtischen Bereich; Bedarf an Rind/pro Jahr: zwischen 2735 und 3650 Stück = Bedarfsdeckung aus dem Umland möglich; kleinster Anteil an Rind im Militärlager; gleicher Anteil an Schwein in der Stadt wie in den ländlichen Siedlungen, entweder dort selbst gezüchtet oder von weiter her importiert; höherer Anteil an Schwein im Militärlager, wahrscheinlich dort selbst gezüchtet.	In Flussauen, Überflutungsbereichen; hauptsächlich Rinder (jüngeres Schlachtalter als in der Stadt), gefolgt von Schaf/Ziege und Schwein; gleicher Anteil an Schwein wie in der Stadt; der Rinderbedarf in der Stadt konnte mit dem Bestand aus dem Umland (3–4 Rinder pro Jahr) gedeckt werden	Archäozoologische Untersuchungen bislang nicht ausreichend publiziert; Strontium-Isotopen-Untersuchungen bisher nicht durchgeführt.	Vor allem Auenlandschaften geeignet für Weideland; Vieharten unbekannt: bisher keine zooarchäologischen Daten wegen fehlenden Knochenmaterials (keine Erhaltung in den vorherrschenden Böden möglich); ländliche Bauweise der Wohn-Stallhäuser und Glöckchenfunde lassen auf Viehhaltung schließen.

Tabelle 1 *(Fortsetzung)*

	Nijmegen	Umland/Hinterland	Xanten	Umland/Hinterland
Gewerbe/lokale Produktion	1. Jh.: lokale Keramikproduktion; Ziegelproduktion.		1. Jh. (vorcolonia-zeitlich): Töpferei, Metallverarbeitung, Beinschnitzerei, Gerberei/Tuchwalkerei, Lederverarbeitung, Leimsiederei, Malerbetriebe, ggf. Brauerei, Metzgerei, Räucherei; 2.–3. Jh.: Abnahme der Produktion? oder Befundzerstörung durch nachantike Steinraubaktivitäten und daher nicht mehr nachweisbar	
überregionale Importartikel	Legionslager (*legio X*): Import von Steinmaterialien, z.B. Grauwacke aus dem Koblenzer Raum, Kalkstein von der Mosel und Tuffe aus der Vulkaneifel; 2. Jh.: Import von Keramik (mit Inhalt, z.B. Fleisch oder Honig). Import von Dinkel, Linse und Erbse aus fruchtbaren Lössgebieten des südlichen Rheinlands; Weizenimport aus Gallien; Datteln, Feigen und Pinie aus dem Mittelmeerraum.		Import von Getreide-sorten wie Dinkel, Emmer, Gerste, Hirse, aus fruchtbaren Löss-gebieten (südliches Rheinland?); Olivenöl und Fischsauce aus Südspanien; Wein aus Italien und Gallien; Keramik; Bauhölzer aus Odenwald und Schwarzwald; Steinmaterialien, z.B. Tuff aus der Vulkaneifel, Marmor aus dem Mittelmeerraum	
Exportartikel	Dachziegel (*villae* und Tempel)		Kein nennenswerter Absatz von vorcoloniazeitlichen Erzeugnissen in der näheren Region	

Tabelle 1 *(Fortsetzung)*

Stones, Tiles, Temples and Villas. A Social-Economic Transformation of the *civitas Batavorum* (85–120 AD)

Harry van Enckevort

Over five decades after the arrival of its legions in the Lower Rhine area, the Roman army made some drastic alterations in their military strategy. Under Caligula and Claudius, an important change was made in the strategy against the Germans, and a linear defence system of *castella* and watchtowers was constructed on the southern bank of the river Rhine.[1] The pressure that this army's presence in the Dutch eastern river area had on the indigenous communities was great. Several sources have revealed that the Batavians provided thousands of men for the Roman *auxilia*.[2] However, this recruitment and the supply of regional nourishment, leather, and other goods had hardly any influence on the Batavian settlements; in any case, the archaeological records do not reflect a marked effect in the architecture of the houses in the countryside. The small farming communities retained their own Batavian ('prehistoric') identity, although a limited number of 'Roman' objects, such as wheel-thrown pottery, coins and militaria did turn up in the settlements during excavations.[3] It is unclear whether these objects represent contacts with the Romans, or if these are goods that were brought home by the soldiers from the *auxillia*. Only the Batavian capital *Oppidum Batavorum*, which was founded by the Romans at the centre of modern Nijmegen ca. 12 BC, shows a development from a road settlement (*vicus*) towards a real Roman town.[4] A similar development, albeit on a much smaller scale, can be seen in *vici* like Cuijk, which was founded around 40 AD.[5] These central places and the *castella* along the Rhine were relatively isolated Roman spots in the hinterland of the limes.

During the Batavian Revolt in 69–70 AD, the rebels set large parts of the limes infrastructure along the Rhine, *Oppidum Batavorum* and the *vicus* of Cuijk, on fire. After the army under the command of Quintus Petillius Cerialis had quashed the revolt, new fortresses were built for *Legio II adiutrix* on the ruins of *Oppidum Batavorum* in 70 AD, and its successor for *Legio X gemina* in the eastern part of Nijmegen in or shortly after 71 AD. In the same period a new capital for the Batavians was founded in the western part of Nijmegen,[6] and on the bank of the Rhine burned down *castella* were repaired and new ones were built with the help of Tenth Legion, as the distribution map of tiles with stamps of this legion shows (fig. 1). In general, the Tenth Legion aimed to supervise and control the movements of people, and to protect the roads and other lines of communication in the Dutch part of the Lower German limes.

The final decades of the 1st century, and especially the first years of the reign of Trajan, were characterised by several important military and administrative modifications. The incorporation of the Lower Rhine zone into the Empire reached its peak when the military district, which was under the rule of the commander of the Lower Rhine army, was transformed into the new province of *Germania inferior* in 85 AD. The decisive

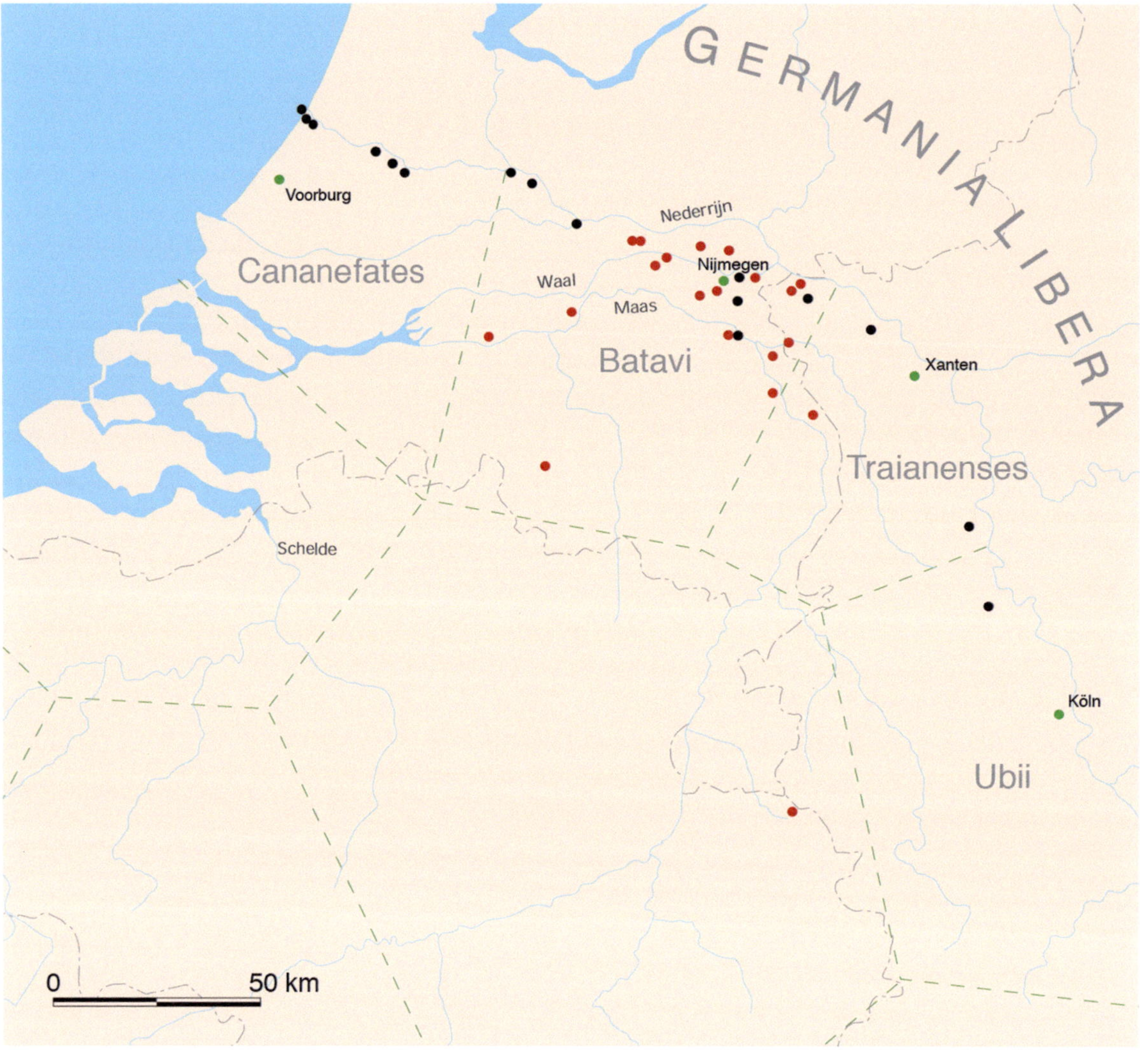

Fig. 1: Distribution map of stamps on roof tiles of the Legio X gemina. green = civitas capital, black = military settlement, red = other settlement.

actions of Trajan, who at the time of his accession of office in 98 AD was in the capital of *Germania inferior* Cologne, accelerated the integration of the frontier *civitates* of the *Batavi* and the *Cananefates*. This is shown, among other things, by the dates of building activities along the limes road in the west of the Netherlands, by the placing of milestones and by the subsequent renovation of the several *castella* during the first years of this emperor's reign.[7]

In that same period, the fortress of the Tenth Legion was rebuilt in stone. The roof tiles were provided by the legion's own tile workhops at De Holdeurn in nearby Berg en Dal. Stone was supplied from further-away quarries, since usable stone did not occur in the Batavian territory. The grauwacke so frequently used in the foundations of buildings in the fortress was imported via the Rhine from the Koblenz area. The limestone for the furnishing of buildings was obtained from Norroy on the Mosel, near Metz in northeastern France, and tufa was extracted in the Brohltal, in the German Eifel. Altar stones found near the quarries show that soldiers of the Tenth Legion were involved in the extraction of both limestone and tufa.[8]

The measures of Marcus Ulpius Traianus also seem to have been very influential in the Roman town of Nijmegen ca. 100 AD. It is likely that the bestowal of municipal rights in the early years of Trajan's reign was intended to promote the definitive integration of the Batavian tribal territory into the Roman Empire, as a *civitas* on the Roman pattern. The new name for the already existing settlement, *Ulpia Noviomagus*, also stems from this period. The existing municipal settlement was transformed into a fully-fledged, Roman-designed administrative centre of the *civitas Batavorum*. The army had the experts and the manpower to design and build inside and outside the fortress. As is evident from the tiles used, the Tenth Legion was actively involved in the construction of the public baths and the public temples in the Batavian capital. Moreover, grauwacke, the stone that was used in many foundations of buildings in the fortress, was also used in the foundations of both buildings. The changes caused by the municipal rights are also clearly noticeable in the range of pottery in the Roman capital. Previously, most domestic pottery had been produced by local potters. From the beginning of the 2nd century, however, the majority of the pottery with contents (meat, honey etc.) seems to have been imported from elsewhere. With regard to pottery, in any case, the consumer function of the town gained precedence over its productive function.[9]

Beside these urban traces, the integration and romanisation processes that were started by Trajan also left clear marks on the Batavian countryside. The continuous military presence of the Tenth Legion in Nijmegen in the years 71–104/105 AD spawned a complex interrelation between the army and Batavian society. The hinterland of *Ulpia Noviomagus* underwent large-scale changes from the end of the 1st century onwards.

The distribution of stamped roof tiles of the Tenth Legion is not limited to the limes zone and Nijmegen, as figure 1 shows. There are indications that the army was involved in the creation of a villa system within the Batavian territory during the Flavian period and the early years of Trajan's reign. Stone buildings are known to have been lacking in the hinterland of Nijmegen in the period that preceded the Batavian Revolt. Batavians were not used to build in stone, since usable stone did not occur in their territory. Only the (Gallo-)Roman architects employed by the Tenth Legion had the necessary know-how to build in stone. It is certain that the tiles were used on the roofs of the most important buildings in villas. Besides these roof tiles, the introduction of other building materials may be seen at settlement sites in the hinterland of Nijmegen. The use of grauwacke in the foundations of several villa buildings in the direct hinterland of Nijmegen is particularly remarkable. The use of the same kind of stone and tiles of the Tenth Legion in various villas in the same period as the stone building phase of the Nijmegen fortress and the public buildings in *Ulpia Noviomagus* suggests that the army took also part in building

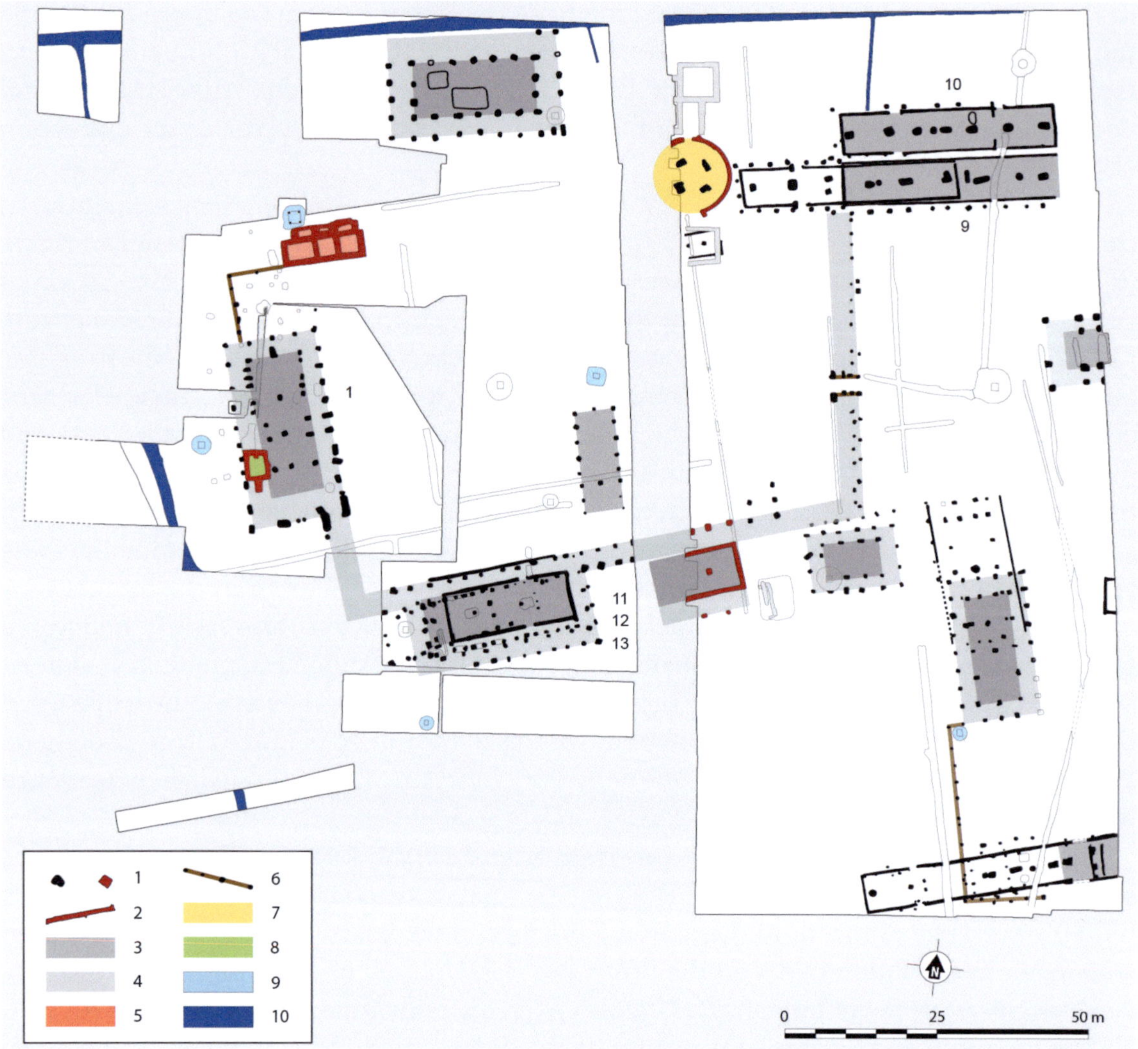

Fig. 2: Plan of the fourth phase of the Druten-Klepperhei villa, mostly timber built, at the beginning of the 2nd century. Features from other phases are not colored. 1 posthole, 2 foundation of gravel or stone, 3 (main) building, 4 portico/colonade, 5 bathhouse, 6 fence, 7 mausoleum, 8 cellar, 9 well, 10 ditch.

activities in the Batavian countryside. In these settlements, production was organised in a rather more Roman manner than before the Batavian Revolt, which allowed for intensification of the agricultural production, especially horse-breeding. The villa owners were probably members of the municipal elite of magistrates and the *ordo decurionum* of *Ulpia Noviomagus*.[10]

The villa of Druten-Klepperhei, ca. 20 km west of Nijmegen, was founded after the Batavian Revolt. Spatial relations between features like postholes of buildings, ditches, fences and wells made it possible to reconstruct the five phases in the development of this villa. In the fourth phase at the beginning of the 2nd century the main building, at the left side in figure 2, is strongly reminiscent of the rectangular indigenous farmhouses. However, the portico on four sides, the stone cellar, wall paintings and a nearby bathhouse with grauwacke foundations clearly reveals a Gallo-Roman architecture style. This building took a central position inside the western part of the settlement, which was laid out in the shape of a square, in which some porticos are extended as a colonnade. Most of the buildings were positioned around this central open space (*pars urbana*). Various other buildings in the eastern part of the settlement, some of which also had a portico, were situated in at least three rows (*pars rustica*). The reconstructed settlement plan shows that this villa, with buildings with walls that are largely made of wattle and daub, should be attributed to the monumental villas of the Anthée type. Phase 3 and 4 of the settlement show yet another remarkable building. Namely, that the villa contains a circular mausoleum, which is positioned on the highest point of the area and partly constructed from grauwacke. This is the first grave monument of this type that was found in or nearby a settlement from the Roman period in the Netherlands. At about the middle of the 2nd century, in phase 5 the villa was replaced by one of the Rhineland type.[11]

Building activities did not remain restricted to the rural settlements, however; traces of construction activities by the Tenth Legion were also found in a number of temple locations, such as Elst-Westeraam, Elst-Centrum and Cuijk. In the summer of 2002, in the course of a rescue excavation on the Westeraam housing development estate to the east of Elst, and 10 km north of Nijmegen, the remains of a temple complex were investigated, which can be dated between 40 and 170 AD. The features, again, can be attributed to five different building phases. In the fourth phase, the wooden temple was replaced by a Gallo-Roman temple of tufa and limestone, with a grauwacke foundation (fig. 3). The use of this latter stone indicates the involvement of the Tenth Legion in the construction of this building, which must have taken place around the year 100.[12]

On the other side of the river, in the centre of the *vicus* Elst, stood a larger monumental, classicised Gallo-Roman temple, which has already been researched extensively by Bogaers in 1955.[13] Its distance to the temple at Elst-Westeraam is about 560 metres. Grauwacke was used in both the first and the second building phase of the temple. The use of this kind of stone in the first phase probably implies that this temple was erected in the Neronian period, over 20 years later than was supposed by Bogaers. In those years grauwacke was used in the fortress on the Fürstenberg in Xanten and in *Oppidum Batavorum*. Bogaers dated the second building phase of the temple at Elst-Centrum immediately after the Batavian Revolt. However, dendrochrological research carried out by archaeologists of the VU University Amsterdam revealed that this temple was not built until ca. 100 AD.[14]

Two fragments of a building inscription show that in the years 98–102 AD, Trajan himself had an indirect hand in the construction or repair of an important building in the *vicus* of Cuijk (15 km south of Nijmegen), as can be deduced from a building inscription.[15] In that same period, a gravelled path was laid close to where this inscription

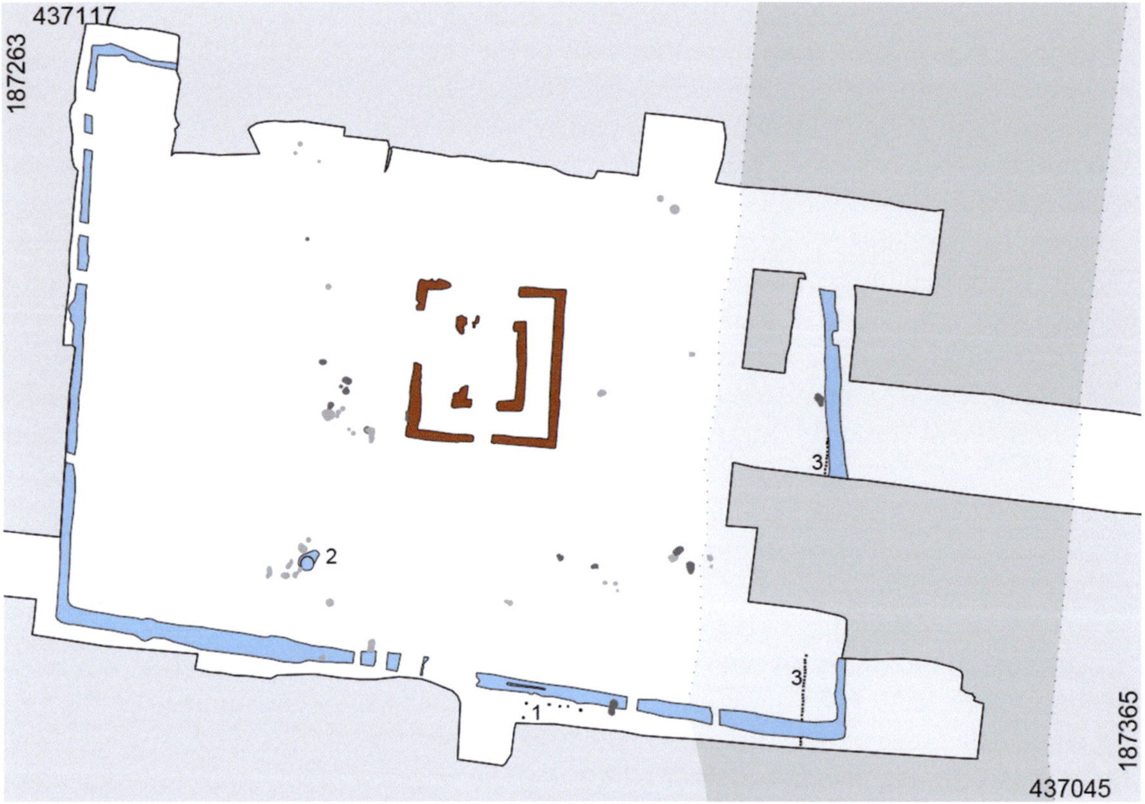

Fig. 3: Plan of the Elst-Westeraam temple with a stone foundation (brown) inside the foundation ditch of a wooden palisade (blue) at the beginning of the 2nd century. 1 small wooden building, 2 well, 3 palisade of pointed, 6–8 centimeters thick stakes rammed into the ground.

was discovered, on both sides of which remains of two Gallo-Roman temples were found. That the Tenth Legion was involved in building activities at Cuijk is also proven by various stamps on roof tiles.[16]

As is evident from the altar stones mentioned before, the extraction of the stone needed for the building activities in the Batavian area seems to have been in the hands of the Tenth Legion. In view of the necessary degree of organisation and infrastructure during the Flavian and early Trajanic period, it is reasonable to assume that the river transport could only have been set up by the army as well. On the basis of this, the excavators of the monumental classicised Gallo-Roman temple of Empel near Hertogenbosch, have concluded that the army, and possibly even the Tenth Legion, was involved in the construction of the building. A votive inscription on a bronze plaque found on site of a veteran of the Tenth Legion, may be a symbol of this connection.[17]

It is remarkable that the hand of Trajan can be spotted, either directly or indirectly, in the construction of public buildings in *Ulpia Noviomagus* and in villas and temples on the

Fig. 4: Front and back of a fragment of a bronze tabella (54 by 47 cm) that was found during the excavations of *Ulpia Noviomagus* on the Weurtseweg.

Batavian countryside. One's sense of his involvement increases as the building activities in the Batavian area are seen in a broader context. This concerns the renovation of the limes road in the west of the Netherlands, the milestones, the subsequent renovation and building of several *castellas* and the reconstruction in stone of the Nijmegen fortress. The building activities that were initiated by Trajan so quickly after his coronation to emperor suggest that there may have been blueprints for these projects already under his predecessor Domitian. This meant that the Batavian civitas was developed to form a strong part of the buffer zone between the rich provinces of Gaul and the Germanic tribes north of the Rhine. Around 104 AD when it appeared that the Tenth Legion could be better deployed in Pannonia, the legion was withdrawn from Nijmegen and directed to Aquincum (Budapest) on the Danube. But the integration of the *civitas Batavorum* did not stop with the departure of the Tenth Legion. Until 122 AD the *vexillatio Britannica* continued the development of the *civitas Batavorum.*[18]

If nowhere else, the continuing romanisation and the resulting integration of the Batavian area in the Roman Empire certainly led to psychological, social and cultural changes among the Batavian aristocracy. These changes are reflected by a fragment of a bronze *tabella* that mentions the name M. Ulpius [- - - at least four times (fig. 4). On the basis of the names of the consuls Servianus and Sura on the back of this *tabella*, the inscription may be dated to January or February of the year 102 AD. The document was signed by a number of Batavian men from the highest social strata. As is clearly shown by the romanised names, these men seem to have been given civil rights by the emperor between the year 98, when Trajan became emperor, and the signing date of the *tabella* in question. Some of the members of this urban upperclass were buried in rich graves near the town. The combination of shield, weapons, *strigili* and writing utensils in one of the graves reflects the Romano-Batavian background of the deceased person.[19]

The use of building materials such as grauwacke and stamped tiles show that, at the beginning of the 2nd century, the army was also involved in the construction of both public buildings in Nijmegen and villas and temples in the Batavian countryside. The construction of these buildings seem rather to have been intended to help expand the infrastructural and administrative structure of the *civitas Batavorum* on the Roman model. In combination with archaeological data about the use of pottery and and the aforementioned *tabella* this suggests an important social-economic transformation of the *civitas Batavorum* during a period of almost less than a generation, between 85 and 122 AD. The reorganisation from a military district on the Lower Rhine into the province of *Germania inferior*, the grant of municipal status and the imperial name to the town, the construction of villas and temples, as well as the substitution of hand-made by wheel thrown pottery, are important signs of this development. Other signs stem from the archaezoological and archaeobotanical research, such as the decline of sheep farming and the rise of horse breeding and changes in arable farming.[20] This illustrates how the social and economic development of the Batavian community could be bound up with the Roman army and the career of Trajan. It is striking that this process started decades after the Rhine was established as the northwestern frontier of the Empire and even 120 years after the arrival of the Romans.

Notes

[1] Willems 1984, 226–240.

[2] Roymans 2004; 2011.

[3] E. g. Nicolay 2007.

[4] Van Enckevort – Heirbaut 2015a, 285–290.

[5] Van Enckevort 2012, 180–186.

[6] Willems – Van Enckevort 2009; Van Enckevort – Heirbaut 2015a, 291–298; 2015b.

[7] Haalebos – Willems 1999; Hessing 1999; Graafstal 2002

[8] Bogaers – Haalebos 1977, 106 f.

[9] Van Enckevort 2012, 269–273; Van Enckevort – Heirbaut 2015a, 291–298.

[10] Van Enckevort 2012, 277–281.

[11] Van Enckevort 2012, 232–245.

[12] Van Enckevort 2012, 197–215.

[13] Bogaers 1955.
[14] Derks et al. 2008; Van Enckevort 2012, 274.
[15] Haalebos 2002.
[16] Van Enckevort 2012, 274.
[17] Roymans et al. 1994, 42–47; Roymans – Derks 1994, 22. 26.
[18] Van Enckevort 2012, 223. 269.
[19] Van Enckevort – Thijssen 2001, 208.
[20] Groot 2008; Groot et al. 2009; Kooistra 2012.

Image Credits

Fig. 1–3: Rob Mols, municipality of Nijmegen. – Fig. 4: André Simons, municipality of Nijmegen.

References

Bogaers 1955
J.E. Bogaers, De Gallo-Romeinse tempels te Elst in de Over-Betuwe, Nederlandse Oudheden I ('s Gravenhage 1955).

Derks et al. 2008
T. Derks – J. Van Kerckhove – P. Hoff (eds.), Nieuw archeologisch onderzoek rond de Grote Kerk van Elst, gemeente Overbetuwe (2002–2003), Zuidnederlandse Archeologische Rapporten 31 (Amsterdam 2008).

Van Enckevort 2012
H. van Enckevort, Gebundelde sporen. Enkele kanttekeningen bij aardewerk en nederzettingen uit Romeins Nederland, Archeologische Berichten Nijmegen 7 (PhD. diss. Leiden University, Nijmegen 2012).

Van Enckevort – Heirbaut 2015a
H. van Enckevort – E. N. A. Heirbaut, Nijmegen, from Oppidum Batavorum to Vlpia Noviomagus, Civitas of the Batavi. Two successive civitas-capitals, in: M. Reddé – W. Van Andringa (eds.), La naissance des capitales de cités en Gaule Chevelue, Gallia 72, 2015, 285–298.

Van Enckevort – Heirbaut 2015b
H. van Enckevort – E. N. A. Heirbaut, The Fortress of Legio II adiutrix (AD 70–71) on the Ruins of Oppidum Batavorum (Nijmegen, NL), in: L. Vagalinski – N. Sharankov (eds.), Proceedings of the 22nd International Congress of Roman Frontier Studies. Ruse, Bulgaria, September 2012, Bulletin of the National Institute of Archaeology 42 (Sofia 2015) 31–36.

Van Enckevort – Thijssen 2001
H. van Enckevort – J.R.A.M. Thijssen, Der Hauptort der Bataver in Nijmegen im 1. Jahrhundert n. Chr. Von Batavodurum und Oppidum Batavorum nach Ulpia Noviomagus, in: G. Precht – N. Zieling (eds.), Genese, Struktur und Entwicklung Römischer Städte im 1. Jahrhundert n. Chr. in Nieder- und Obergermanien, Xantener Berichte 9 (Xanten 2001) 87–110.

Graafstal 2012
E. P. Graafstal, Logistiek, communicatie en watermanagement. Over de uitrusting van de Romeinse rijksgrens in Nederland, Westerheem 51, 2002, 2–27.
Groot 2008
M. Groot, Surplus Production of Animal Products for the Roman Army in a Rural Settlement in the Dutch River Area, in: S. Stallibrass - R. Thomas (eds.), Feeding the Roman Army. The Archaeology of Production and Supply in NW Europe (Oxford 2008) 83–98.
Groot et al. 2009
M. Groot - S. Heeren - L.I. Kooistra - W. Vos, Surplus Production for the Market? The Agrarian Economy in the Non-villa Landscapes of Germania inferior, JRA 22, 2009, 231–252.
Haalebos 2002
J.K. Haalebos, Een belangrijke bouwinscriptie, in: H. van Enckevort - J.R.A.M. Thijssen (eds.), Cuijk. Een regionaal centrum in de Romeinse tijd, Archeologische Berichten Nijmegen. Monografie 5 (Utrecht 2002) 33–36.
Haalebos - Willems 1999
J.K. Haalebos - W.J.H. Willems, Recent Research on the Limes in the Netherlands, JRA 12, 1999, 247–262.
Hessing 1999
W.A.M. Hessing, Building Programmes for the Lower Rhine Limes. The Impact of the Visits of Trajan and Hadrian to the Lower Rhine, in: H. Sarfatij - W.J.H. Verwers - P.J. Woltering (eds.), In Discussion with the Past. Archaeological Studies Presented to W.A. van Es (Zwolle 1999) 149–156.
Kooistra 2012
L.I. Kooistra, Die pflanzlichen Grundnahrungsmittel der Rheinarmee vor und nach der Gründung der Germania inferior, in: A. Stobbe - U. Tegtmeier (Hrsg.), Verzweigungen. Eine Würdigung für A.J. Kalis und J. Meurers-Balke, Frankfurter Archäologische Schriften 18 (Bonn 2012) 171–187.
Nicolay 2007
J. Nicolay, Armed Batavians. Use and Significance of Weaponry and Horse Gear from Non-military Contexts in the Rhine Delta, 50 BC to AD 450, Amsterdam Archaeological Studies 11 (Amsterdam 2007).
Roymans 2004
N. Roymans, Ethnic Identity and Imperial Power. The Batavians in the Early Roman Empire, Amsterdam Archaeological Studies 10 (Amsterdam 2004).
Roymans 2011
N. Roymans, Etnic Recruitment, Returning Veterans and the Diffusion of Roman Culture among Rural Populations in the Rhineland Frontier Zone, in: N. Roymans - T. Derks (eds.), Villa Landscapes in the Roman North. Economy, Culture and Lifestyles, Amsterdam Archaeological Studies 17 (Amsterdam 2011) 139–160.
Roymans - Derks 1994
N. Roymans - T. Derks, Het heiligdom te Empel. Algemene beschouwingen, in: N. Roymans - T. Derks (eds.), De tempel van Empel. Een Hercules-heiligdom in het woongebied van de Bataven, Graven naar het Brabantse verleden 2 ('s-Hertogenbosch 1994) 10–38.

Roymans et al. 1994

N. Roymans - T. Derks - A. Klomp, Het Gallo-Romeinse tempelcomplex, in: N. Roymans - T. Derks (eds.), De tempel van Empel. Een Hercules-heiligdom in het woongebied van de Bataven, Graven naar het Brabantse verleden 2 ('s-Hertogenbosch 1994) 40–57.

Willems 1984

W.J.H. Willems, Romans and Batavians. A Regional Study in the Dutch Eastern River Area, BerOudhBod 34, 1984, 39–331.

Willems - Van Enckevort 2009

W.J.H. Willems - H. van Enckevort, Vlpia Noviomagvs. Roman Nijmegen. The Batavian Capital at the Imperial Frontier, JRA Suppl. 73 (Portsmouth 2009).

Supplying Food to *Ulpia Noviomagus Batavorum*

Laura I. Kooistra – Maaike Groot

Introduction

Researchers have long assumed that the economic stimulus in the Batavian area (fig. 1) was mainly caused by the recruitment of Batavian young men for the army. This was based on a text by Tacitus, in which it was mentioned that the Batavians were exempt from taxation due to their supply of troops to the Roman army.[1] Nevertheless, the agrarian countryside of the *civitas Batavorum* would also have been drawn into economic change as a result of the demand for agrarian products. That demand was not just from the Roman army, which was especially prominent with the presence of the tenth legion in Nijmegen in the first and early second century.[2] Already in the first century, Nijmegen had a civil centre, *Oppidum Batavorum*, which was strongly connected to the army. This capital of the Batavians was destroyed in 69 AD. After quiet had been restored, a new town was built somewhat to the west along the river Waal; this town received market rights and the name *Ulpia Noviomagus Batavorum* from Emperor Trajan in the early second century AD. The population of this town is estimated at 5,000 to 6,000 civilians. Army and civilian population together at the end of the first century consisted of ca. 10,000 consumers. How were the town and the army supplied and what role did the Batavian rural population play in this supply? These are the questions central to this paper.

Civitas Batavorum

The tribal area of the Batavians was located between the rivers Rhine and Meuse. To the west it was bordered by an extensive peat area, which was part of the territory of the Cananefatians. The eastern border was just to the east of Nijmegen. Most of the Batavian area consisted of low-lying, fertile river deposits. Active rivers with natural levees, alluvial ridges with residual channels and flood basins were the characteristic landscape elements. Only to the south of Nijmegen did high and dry sandy and loamy soils occur. The population outside the town and army camps mainly lived in small agrarian settlements, consisting of one to five wooden byres (fig. 2). Villa-like settlements were scarce;[3] most of them were situated in the vicinity of Nijmegen. The *civitas Batavorum* was relatively densely populated.[4] Vossen argued that more or less 1000 agrarian settlements were contemporaneous in the second century. The settlements were situated on alluvial ridges. Arable farming took place on the alluvial ridges, mainly just above the water level, and the animals were raised mainly in the flood basins.[5]

Fig. 1: Locations of legionary fortresses and cities (large squares) and of attested and presumed smaller forts (small squares) on the left bank of the river Rhine at about AD 100. The *civitas Batavorum* was situated in the river area.

Fig. 2: A reconstruction drawing of Tiel Passewaaij, a rural settlement in *civitas Batavorum.*

Supplying Animal Food to Nijmegen

Animal husbandry in the rural *civitas Batavorum* relied heavily on cattle. Of the three main meat-providing animals, cattle is the most common species, followed by sheep or goat and then pig (fig. 3A). When this is compared with species proportions in Nijmegen, it is clear that cattle shows the highest proportions in the urban assemblages and the lowest in the military ones (fig. 3B–C). Pig frequencies are similar for rural sites and urban Nijmegen, while they are much higher in some of the military assemblages. Since these are the earliest military sites, it seems highly unlikely that the pigs could have been supplied from the surrounding countryside, which had no strong tradition of pig keeping.

Slaughter ages of cattle show that more adult cattle are found in Nijmegen than in the countryside (fig. 4). It seems that cattle were selectively supplied to Nijmegen, with the youngest animals consumed in the countryside and older animals in town. This suggests that there was no system of specialised meat production; otherwise a selection of younger cattle would be expected for the towns.

The size of cattle increases during the Roman period (fig. 5). This would have resulted in higher output, both of traction power and meat.

The animal remains from rural sites in the *civitas Batavorum* and military and civil sites in Nijmegen not only provide information about possible supply, but also about

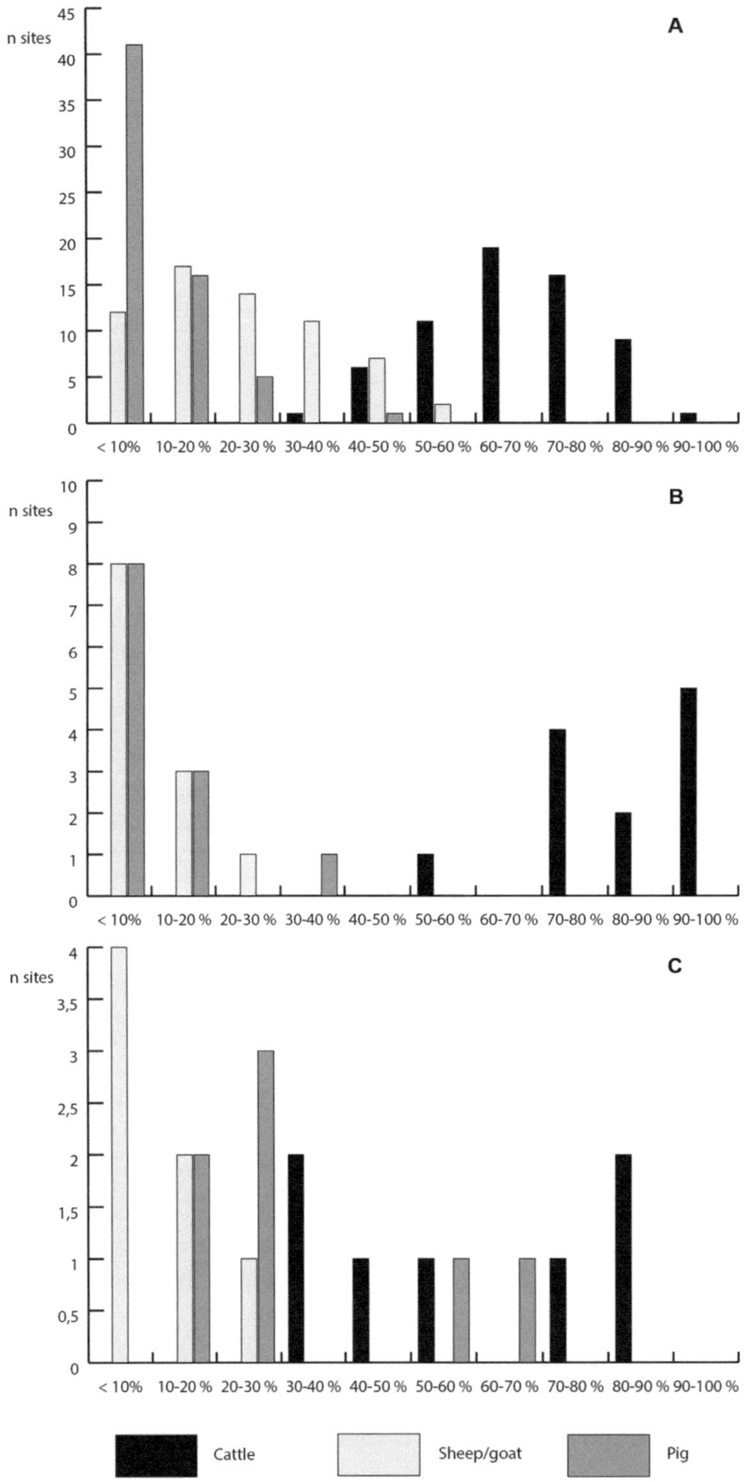

Fig. 3: Species proportions for the main meat-providing livestock species for the rural *civitas Batavorum*, military and civilian Nijmegen (all periods).

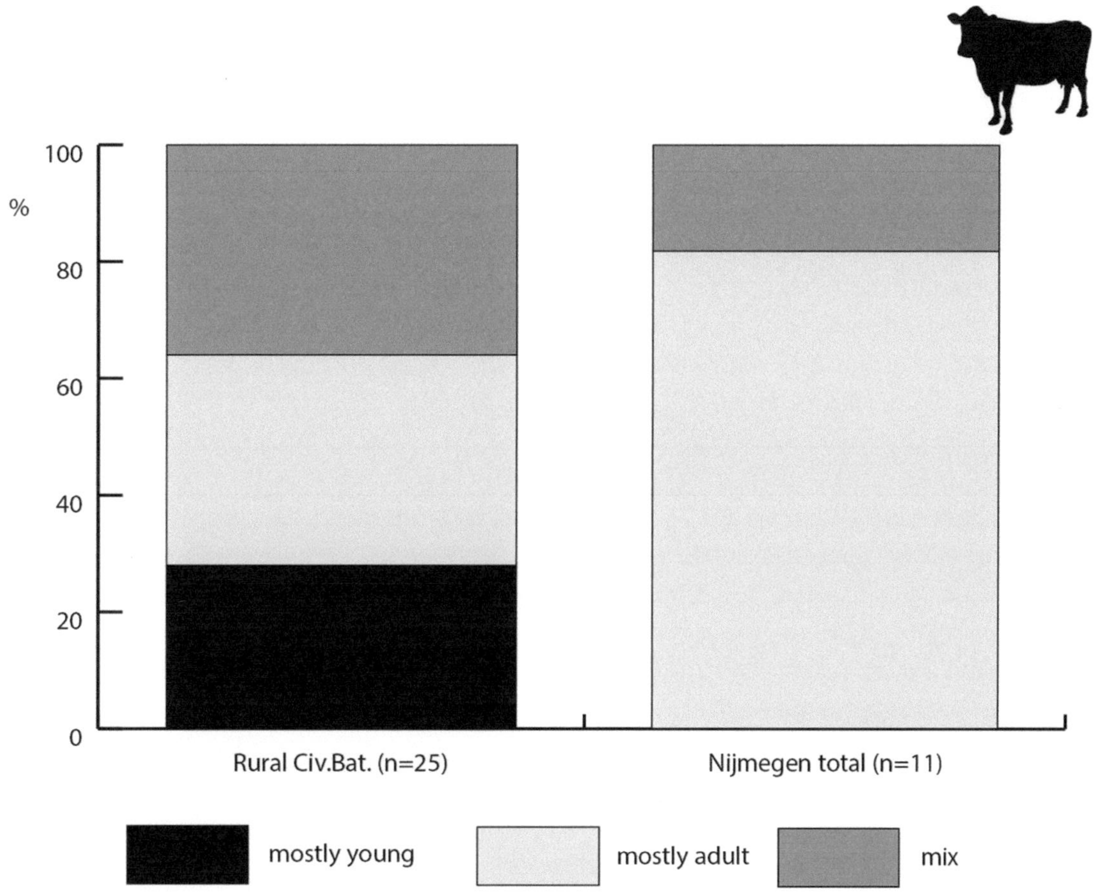

Fig. 4: Slaughter ages for cattle in the rural *civitas Batavorum* and in Nijmegen (military and civilian). For methodology, see Groot – Deschler-Erb 2015.

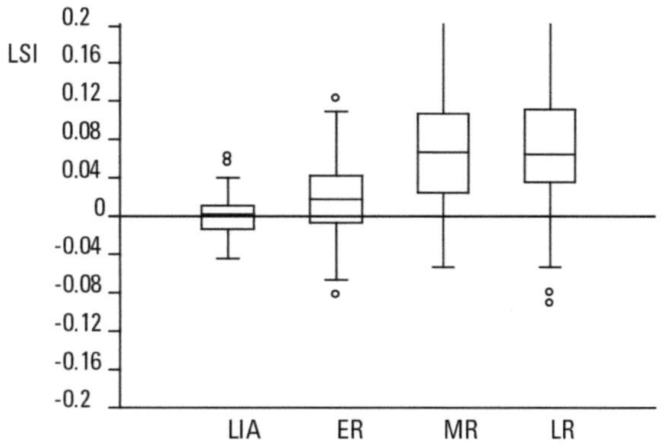

Fig. 5: Logarithmic Scale Index for width measurements for cattle for rural sites from the *civitas Batavorum*, per period. LIA: Late Iron Age, n=63; ER: Early Roman period, n=98; MR: Middle Roman period, n=215; LR: Late Roman period, n=152.

the kind of interaction between the producers and consumers. We find similar species proportions (although with small differences) in producer and consumer sites. In the consumer sites, both young and older animals are represented, and all body parts are present. These are all indicators for direct distribution.[6] Typical for direct distribution is that the farmer is in control of supply, and herd security will always be the farmer's main priority. The distance between farmer and consumer is small, and it is unlikely that there were middlemen operating. Small-scale transactions directly between farmer and consumer are to be expected.

Using the estimated population of Nijmegen around 100 AD, we can reconstruct the amount of meat needed to feed the town. This will help us understand the magnitude of meat production that was required to feed the town and army and conclude whether this was feasible for the rural *civitas Batavorum*. Two different ways of estimating the number of cattle required are used. First, the assumption that people on average consumed about 10% meat in their diet. Second, the assumption that people consumed about 200 grams of meat per day. In the first approach, using the figures from Groot et al. 2009, and assuming that all meat came from cattle to simplify matters, 2735 animals would have been needed per year to feed a military and urban population of Nijmegen consisting of 10,000 people. In the second approach, assuming a meat yield of 200 kg per cattle, and again assuming all meat came from cattle, 3650 cattle were needed per year.[7] The two methods give different results but are of the same order of magnitude. Earlier research suggested that the settlement of Tiel-Passewaaij was able to produce a surplus of 7–40 cattle per year (depending on the period).[8] Although the lowest number does not sound like very much, if we take into account the large number of Roman settlements known for the *civitas Batavorum* (1000), together the settlements could easily have produced enough meat to feed Nijmegen without the need for imported animals or preserved meat. Each settlement would only have needed to supply 3 or 4 cattle per year, which means perhaps 1 animal per family. The animals were probably taken to the market in Nijmegen by their owners or a representative from the village; periodic livestock sales were held in the large structure adjacent to the *canabae legionis*.[9]

Although local supply of meat was possible, this does not mean that there would not have been any non-local supply of meat to Nijmegen. Considering the low proportions of pig in the rural sites, pigs were perhaps either raised in the town or supplied from further away, as live animals or as joints of meat. For the early Roman military occupation on the Kops Plateau, zooarchaeological data suggest that at least some of the cattle consumed there were not local. Measurements of cattle bones indicate that the cattle on the Kops Plateau were larger than those in contemporary rural sites and urban Nijmegen (fig. 6). There is no evidence suggesting different male to female ratios among the cattle in the different sites, so it seems the size difference represents two different populations, with cattle from outside the region represented in the Kops Plateau population.

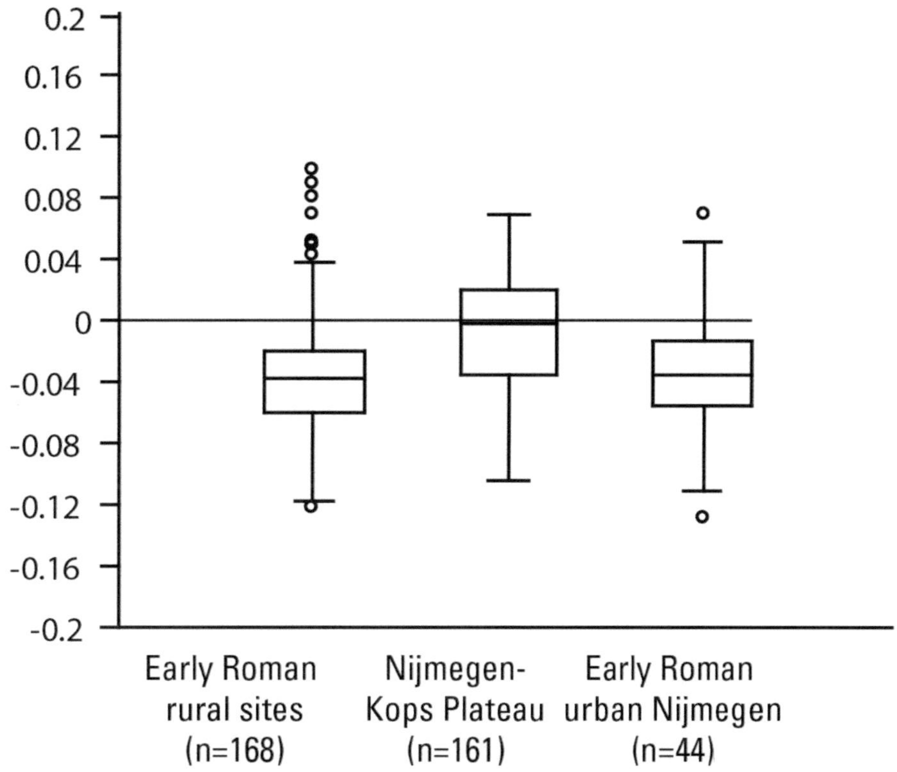

Fig. 6: Logarithmic Scale Index for cattle measurements from Early Roman rural sites in the Central Netherlands, Nijmegen-Kops Plateau and urban Nijmegen.

Supplying Plant Food to Nijmegen

The archaeobotanical data for Nijmegen are mainly derived from military sites (table 1).[10] In addition, soil samples for archaeobotanical research have been taken during several excavations in the town *Ulpia Noviomagus*. These are accessed but not yet analysed.[11] The Romans liked to eat bread, and small pieces of bread were found at Nijmegen (fig. 7). The wheat species bread wheat, spelt wheat and emmer wheat are the species suitable for making bread. Besides these bread-making cereals 50% of the cereals found could be added to flour, but these species do not make bread on their own. These species are barley, millet, oat and rye. Cereal production must have taken place outside the capital and military sites of Nijmegen. Pulses like Celtic bean, lentil and pea, herbs like dill and collected fruit and nuts like bramble, elder, sloe and hazelnut, could have been cultivated in gardens or orchards inside *Ulpia Noviomagus*. There is evidence for orchards, because pruned wood from probably apple or pear, cherry or plum, hazel, peach and raspberry is found in a depression behind houses in *Ulpia Noviomagus* dated in the second century AD.[12] If there are orchards, why not also gardens for products like herbs, vegetables and pulses?

	Augustan base Hunerberg	Oppidum Batavorum	Castra & cannabae legionis	Ulpia Noviomagus houses	Ulpia Noviomagus temples	Civitas Batavorum rural settlements
	19–16/12 BC	before AD 69	end 1st – early 2nd	end 1st – 2nd	end 1st – 2nd	1st – 2nd
	6 samples	inventory (1 site)	37 samples	inventory (5 sites)	2 temples	22 settlements
Cereals						
Barley	4	.	15	2×	1×	21
(Cultivated) Oat	2	1×	10	.	1×	20
Millet	1	.	4	.	.	11
Rye	.	1×	1	.	.	2
Bread Wheat	.	.	7	2×	.	.
Emmer Wheat	1	.	7	.	.	21
Spelt Wheat	.	.	5	.	.	1(ER)
Wheat, not identified	1	1×	10	1×	1×	.
Bread fragments	.	.	3	.	.	.
Food fragments	.	.	2	.	.	.
Pulses						
Celtic Bean	.	.	2	1×	.	7
Lentil	1	1×	3	2×	.	1
Pea	.	.	5	1×	1×	1
Pea/Celtic Bean	1	.	.	.	.	.
Herbs and vegetables						
Aniseed	.	.	1	.	.	.
Beet	.	.	.	.	.	5
Coriander	.	.	1	.	.	5
Dill	.	.	2	.	.	4
cf. Summer Savory	.	.	1	.	.	.

Table 1: The presence of food plants in military and civil sites in Nijmegen and in rural settlements in the *civitas Batavorum*. ER = Early Roman period (1st century AD), cf. = identification not sure.

	Augustan base Hunerberg	Oppidum Batavorum	Castra & cannabae legionis	Ulpia Noviomagus houses	Ulpia Noviomagus temples		Civitas Batavorum rural settlements
Cultivated fruit and nuts							
Apple	.	.	2	.	.		.
Apple/Pear	.	.	1	2×	.		.
Cherry/Plum	.	.	.	1×	.		.
Date	.	.	.	.	1×		.
Fig	.	1×	2	2×	1×		.
Grape	.	.	3	2×	.		.
Hazelnut	1	.	1	.	1×		5
Olive	2	.	1	.	.		.
Peach	.	.	.	1×	.		.
Pear	.	.	2	.	.		.
Plum	.	.	2	1×	.		4
Raspberry	.	.	.	1×	.		2
Stone pine	.	.	.	.	1×		.
Walnut	.	.	1	.	.		2
Wild Cherry/ Sour Cherry	.	.	1	1×	.		.
Collected nuts and fruit							
Blackberry	.	.	.	2×	.		.
Bramble	.	.	1	.	.		3
Dewberry	.	.	1	.	.		2
Elder	.	.	1(cf.)	1×(cf.)	.		11
Sloe	.	.	3	.	.		2
Oil-rich seeds							
Cabbage/ Mustard	.	.	1	.	.		13
Cultivated Flax	1	.	1	.	.		12
Gold-of-pleasure	1	.	1	.	.		8

Table 1 *(continued)*.

Fig. 7: Charred piece of bread found in a water well of a Flavian military site at Nijmegen.

When we compare the food products found at 22 agrarian sites situated in the *civitas Batavorum* with those in Nijmegen, the following remarks can be made. Of the bread-making cereals only emmer wheat could have been supplied by the farmers of *civitas Batavorum*, together with the non-bread cereals as barley, millet and oat. These species were found in the rural settlements and it is likely that these cereals were supplied by the local farmers. For the other plant products found in rural sites of the *civitas Batavorum*, such as pulses – mainly Celtic bean is found – herbs and vegetables, collected and cultivated fruit and nuts, it is not clear (yet) if these products were supplied by the Batavian farmers. There is no doubt that plant foods were delivered from other parts of the Roman Empire. The loess area in the south of *Germania inferior* produced tons of spelt wheat.[13] It is possible that the lentil and pea found in Nijmegen were delivered by the farmers of the loess area, although these species were found just a couple of years ago in a rural settlement on the other side of the river Waal in features dated to the Iron Age (500 to 12 BC, pea) and the first century AD (lentil).[14] There is one more agrarian settlement with pea, dated in the first and second century AD.[15] Bread wheat did not occur in the area of the Batavians and hardly existed in the loess area. This cereal must have been imported from other provinces of the Roman Empire, most likely Gaul. These long-distance cereals were probably brought in by traders, as testified by an inscription found at Nijmegen referring to the Nervian grain trader M. Liberius Victor.[16]

The excavations at Nijmegen also revealed some interesting exotic products that must have been imported from the Mediterranean. The most exciting ones are the concentrations of dates, figs and stone pine nuts found in second-century offering pits adjacent to the temple dedicated to the goddess Fortuna.[17]

The provenance of plant food in military sites and *Ulpia Noviomagus* is rather complex and the connections between farmer and citizen/soldier are not clear yet. What we do know is that several of the plant food species found in rural sites and in Nijmegen are the same (see table 1). This suggests that these products were supplied to Nijmegen by the Batavians. The second strand of evidence, which points to local surplus production of cereals is the increase in storage capacity at some, but not at all, rural sites from the first century until the end of the second century. It is suggested that cereals were stored in central places before transport to Nijmegen or the Roman forts along the Rhine.[18] The third type of evidence to prove surplus production of cereals are calculations based on the availability of arable fields per rural settlement in combination with the labour availability.

To get an idea about the theoretical production capacity of cereals of the Batavian farmers some rough calculations were done, starting from the consumers at Nijmegen. At the end of the first century AD the urban and military population is estimated at ca. 10,000 people, of which 5000 soldiers. Calculations are based on the assumptions that diet contained 70% cereals and that only 50% of the required cereals (only emmer wheat and the non-bread cereals) came from the *civitas Batavorum.*[19] That means that over 1.2×10^6 kilo cereals per year were needed to feed the Nijmegen population.[20] Calculations based on available arable fields, the total of rural settlements and labour in harvest time suggest that theoretically, 7.5×10^6 kilo cereals per year could have been produced as a surplus by the farmers of the *civitas Batavorum.*[21]

All in all, it seems likely that the production capacity was dependent on the population density of the Batavian countryside. Many small-scale producers were theoretically very well able to deliver half of the cereal demand of the civilian and military population.

Conclusion

The conclusions of our study are that the Batavian farmers were able to produce a considerable surplus of cattle and cereals. The surplus production per rural settlement was small, but the amount of settlements was high, which could have ended in a considerable supply of food to the civilian and military population of Nijmegen. The animal food consisted of small-scale transactions between farmers and consumers rather than merchants and traders operating at a large scale. In case of food plants, there could have been a centralisation of cereal storage at the somewhat larger rural sites. It is still unknown if the farmers or the military were responsible for cereal transport to the city or that traders were active in the *civitas Batavorum* as was the case for the long-distance cereal transport.

Notes

[1] Tacitus Germania 29; Historiae IV.12, 17.

[2] Willems 1990, 71; Willems – Van Enckevort 2009, 74.

[3] Vos 2009.

[4] Vossen 2003.

[5] Groot – Kooistra 2009.

[6] Zeder 1991, 36–43.

[7] Based on the highest figure Lepetz uses to calculate meat consumption in Arras (50–200 g per person per day) but adjusting the meat yield per animal, since cattle in the civitas Batavorum were considerably smaller than the cattle in Gaul. Lepetz 1996, 137–138. See also Groot 2016, 224–225.

[8] Groot et al. 2009.

[9] Driessen 2018.

[10] Augustan camp Hunerberg (5 samples) De Hing – Kooistra 1995; Mid-first century camp Kops Plateau (1 sample) Buurman 1988; Flavian *castra* and *canabae legionaris* location Canisiuscollege (37 samples) Buurman 1984 (1 sample); De Hingh – Kooistra 1995 & unpublished data (35 samples); Kooistra 1989 (1 sample).

[11] Hänninen – Vermeeren 1995.

[12] Van Rijn 1998; context information and dating from Harry van Enckevort.

[13] Kooistra 1996; Schamuhn – Zerl 2009.

[14] Kooistra – Kubiak-Martens 2016.

[15] Lange 1990.

[16] Driessen 2007, 161. 177–178 fig. 85.

[17] Hänninen – Vermeeren 1997.

[18] Groot et al. 2009.

[19] Groot et al. 2009; Kooistra 2012; Van Dinter et al. 2014. We calculated with 10% meat, 70% cereals and 20% other food products.

[20] Based on 5000 soldiers (3000 kcal/person), and a civil population of 833 men, 833 women (2200 kcal/person), 833 subadult men (10–14 years old, 2750 kcal), 833 subadult women (same age, 2420 kcal/person), 833 children (1–4 years old, 1360 kcal/person) and 833 small children (0–1 years old, 550 kcal/person). The energy needs mentioned after Gregg 1988, 143. It is assumed that 1 kg cereals provides 3100 kcal of energy (Bloemers 1978, 70; Bakels 1982, 10).

[21] Based on 1000 rural settlements (Vossen – Groot 2008; Vos 2009, 209–216) with 2.5 families per settlement in average (Vos 2009, 215), 5–8 persons per family (Bloemers 1978, 55; Willems 1984, 236) and the same proportions of adults and children as the civil population. It is assumed that each settlement had 30–40 ha of arable fields (Groot et al. 2009). With the assumption of 70% cereal needs the rural population needed 3×10^6 kg cereals per year. Therefore almost 10,000 ha arable fields were in use (assumed yield 1000 kg cereals/ha, 200 kg of sowing-seed, and 200 kg in reserve, and a two-course rotation system). The calculation of surplus is based on labour capacity in harvest time (14 days a year and each man could harvest 0.25 ha/day). The calculated 4062.50 men are theoretically able to harvest cereals from more than 14,000 ha/year, from which ca. 5000 ha for own purpose and 9000 ha for surplus. With 800 kg cereals/ha (200 kept aside for sowing-seed) a theoretical surplus of 7.5×10^6 kg cereals/year is possible.

Image Credits

Fig. 1: after Polak and Kooistra 2015, fig. 1. – Fig. 2: Mikko Kriek. – Fig. 3–4: Maaike Groot. – Fig. 5: Groot 2016, fig. 5.49. – Fig. 6: Groot 2018, fig. 6. – Fig. 7: BIAX *Consult.*

References

Bakels 1982

C.C. Bakels, Zum wirtschaftlichen Nutzungsraum einer bandkeramischen Siedlung, in: Siedlungen der Kultur mit Linearkeramik in Europa (Nitra 1982) 9–16.

Bloemers 1978

J.H.F. Bloemers, Rijswijk (Z.H.), `De Bult': Eine Siedlung der Cananefaten, Nederlandse Oudheden 8 (Amersfoort 1978).

Buurman 1984

J. Buurman, Botanisch laboratorium, Jaarverslag Rijksdienst voor het Oudheidkundig Bodemonderzoek 1982, 1984, 91–94.

Buurman 1988

J. Buurman, Botanisch laboratorium, Jaarverslag Rijksdienst voor het Oudheidkundig Bodemonderzoek 1987, 1988, 86–89.

Van Dinter et al. 2014

M. van Dinter – L. I. Kooistra – M. K. Dütting – P. van Rijn – C. Cavallo, Could the Local Population of the Lower Rhine Delta Supply the Roman Army? Part 2: Modelling the Carrying Capacity of the Delta Using Archaeological, Palaeo-Ecological and Geomorphological Data, Journal of Archaeology in the Low Countries 5, 2014, 5–50.

Driessen 2007

M.J. Driessen, Bouwen om te blijven: De topografie, bewonings¬continuïteit en monumentaliteit van Romeins Nijmegen, Rapportage Archeologische Monumentenzorg 151 (Amersfoort 2007).

Driessen 2018

M. Driessen, Nice Meating: The canabae legionis Livestock Market at Nijmegen Revisited, in: T. Ivleva – J. de Bruin – M. Driessen (eds), Embracing the Provinces. Society and Material Culture of the Roman Frontier Regions. Essays in Honour of Dr Carol van Driel-Murray (Oxford 2018) 121–132.

Gregg 1988

S.A. Gregg, Foragers and Farmers: Population Interaction and Argicultural Expansion in Prehistoric Europe (Chicago 1988).

Groot 2016

M. Groot, Livestock for Sale. Animal Husbandry in a Roman Frontier Zone, Amsterdam Archaeological Studies 24 (Amsterdam 2016).

Groot 2018

M. Groot, How to Feed a Roman Camp, in: S. Matesic – C.S. Sommer (eds), Limes XXIII: Proceedings of the 23rd International Limes Congress Ingolstadt 2015, Beiträge zum Welterbe Limes Sonderband 4 (Mainz 2018) 971–977.

Groot – Deschler-Erb 2015

M. Groot – E. Deschler-Erb, Market Strategies in the Roman Provinces: Different Animal Husbandry Systems Explored by a Comparative Regional Approach, JASc: Reports 4, 2015, 447–460.

Groot et al. 2009

M. Groot – S. Heeren – L.I. Kooistra – W. Vos, Surplus Production for the Market? The Agrarian Economy in the non-villa landscapes of Germania Inferior, Journal of Roman Archaeology 22, 2009, 231–252.

Groot – Kooistra 2009

M. Groot – L.I. Kooistra, Land Use and the Agrarian Economy in the Roman Dutch River Area, Internet Archaeology 27, 2009, 1–53.

Hänninen – Vermeeren 1995

K. Hänninen – C. Vermeeren, Het karakter van Nijmegen. Een overzicht van de karakterisering van zadenmonsters van de Biezenstraat, Gerard Noodtstraat, Hessenberg, Kruisweg, Maasplein, Piersonstraat en Rivierstraat en het onderzoek aan hout van de opgravingen Hessenberg, Gerard Noodtstraat, Maasplein, Rivierstraat en Weurtse weg, BIAXrapport 10 (Amsterdam 1995).

Hänninen – Vermeeren 1997

K. Hänninen – C. Vermeeren, Exotische offers. Botanisch onderzoek aan kuilen uit de Romeinse Fortuna-tempel op het Maasplein in Nijmegen, BIAXiaal 51 (Amsterdam 1997).

De Hingh – Kooistra 1995

A.E. de Hingh – L.I. Kooistra, Reste von Getreide und anderen Pflanzen, in: J. K. Haalebos (Hrsg.): Castra und Canabae; Ausgrabungen auf dem Hunerberg in Nijmegen 1987–1994, Libelli Noviomagenses 3 (Nijmegen 1995) 103–109.

Kooistra 1989

L.I. Kooistra, Botanische resten uit een kuil, bijlage bij, in: J.E. Bogaers – J.K. Haalebos (eds.), Opgravingen op het terrein van het voormalige Canisiuscollege, 1988, Numaga 36 (Mijmegen 1989) 58–60.

Kooistra 1996

L.I. Kooistra, Borderland Farming. Possibilities and Limitations of Farming in the Roman Period and the Early Middle Ages between the Rhine and Meuse (Assen 1996).

Kooistra 2012

L.I. Kooistra, Die pflanzlichen Grundnahrungsmittel der Rheinarmee vor und nach der Gründung der Germania inferior, in: A. Stobbe – U. Tegtmeier (Hrsg.), Verzweigungen. Eine Würdigung (Bonn 2012) 171–187.

Kooistra – Kubiak-Martens 2016

L.I. Kooistra – L. Kubiak-Martens, Botanisch onderzoek, in: E.N.A. Heirbaut – C.W. Koot (red.), Archeologische monumentenzorg in het plangebied van de dijkteruglegging bij Lent 4. Archeologisch onderzoek naar vindplaats 9/57 en de bewoningsgeschiedenis van de ijzertijd en de Romeinse tijd deel II, Archeologische Berichten Nijmegen – Rapport 61 (Nijmegen 2016) 841–856.

Lange 1990

A.G. Lange, De Horden near Wijk bij Duurstede. Plant Remains from a Native Settlement at the Roman Frontier: a Numerical Approach, Nederlandse Oudheden 13 (Amersfoort 1990).

Lepetz 1996

S. Lepetz, L`animal dans la société Gallo-romaine de la France du Nord (Amiens 1996).

Polak – Kooistra 2015

M. Polak – L.I. Kooistra, A Sustainable Frontier? The Establishment of the Roman Frontier in the Rhine Delta. Part 1: From the End of the Iron Agee to the Death of Tiberius (c. 50 BC–AD 37), Jahrbuch des Römisch-Germanischen Zentralmuseums Mainz 60. Jahrgang 2013, 2015, 355–458.

Van Rijn et al. 1998.

P. van Rijn – K. Hänninen – C. Vermeeren, Hout van Nijmegen gebundeld. Houtonderzoek van Nijmegen van de Romeinse vindplaats Weurtse Weg en de post-middeleeuwse opgravingen van Hessenberg, Hezelstraat en Waalkade, BIAXiaal 70 (Amsterdam 1998).

Schamuhn – Zerl 2009

S. Schamuhn – T. Zerl, Zur Landwirtschaft der Kelten, Römer und Germanen im Gebiet von Nordrhein-Westfalen. Kontinuität oder Wandel?, in: S. Zimmer (ed.), Kelten am Rhein. Akten des Dreizehnten Internationalen Keltologiekongresses / Proceedings of the Thirteenth International Congress of Celtic Studies, 23. bis 27. Juli 2007 in Bonn. 1. Archäologie – Ethnizität und Romanisierung, BJb Beih. 58,1 (Mainz 2009) 239–250.

Vos 2009

W.K. Vos, Bataafs platteland: Het Romeinse nederzettingslandschap in het Nederlandse Kromme-Rijngebied, Nederlandse Archeologische Rapporten 35 (Amersfoort 2009).

Vossen 2003

I.M.J. Vossen, The Possibilities and Limitations of Demographic Calculations in the Batavian Area, in: Th. Grünewald – S. Seibel (Hrsg.), Kontinuität und Diskontinuität. Germania inferior am Beginn und am Ende der römischen Herrschaft, Reallexikon der Germanischen Altertumskunde Ergänzungsband 35 (Berlin 2003) 414–435.

Willems 1984

W.J.H. Willems, Romans and Batavians: A Regional Study in the Dutch Eastern River Area, II, Berichten van de Rijksdienst voor het Oudheidkundig Bodemonderzoek 34, 1984, 39–331.

Willems 1990

W.J.H. Willems, Romeins Nijmegen. Vier eeuwen stad en centrum aan de Waal (Utrecht 1990).

Willems – Van Enckevort 2009

W.J.H. Willems – H. van Enckevort (eds), Ulpia Noviomagus, Roman Nijmegen: The Batavian capital at the imperial frontier, Portsmouth, JRA Suppl. 73 (Rhode Island 2009).

Zeder 1991

M.A. Zeder, Feeding Cities: Specialized Animal Economy in the Ancient Near East, Smithsonian Series in Archaeological Inquiry (Washington 1991).

Colonia Ulpia Traiana: The Economy of a Garrison and Border Town at the Lower German Limes

Christoph Eger

Around AD 100, Emperor Trajan granted the rights of a colony to a settlement on the northeastern border of the province of *Germania Inferior*, which was not known by name.[1] *Colonia Ulpia Traiana* (CUT), as the city was known from then on, was located on the west bank of the Rhine above a bluff slope. Presumably, the favourable location for a river port was the decisive factor for the creation of a civilian settlement here, in Tiberian times at the latest. Its development was intimately linked to the legionnaires' camp Vetera, which was located farther south, on the Fürstenberg. Vetera had been built around 13/12 BC. In a strategic position, opposite the confluence of the Lippe and the Rhine, it had been established as a base camp for the campaigns of Drusus and Tiberius. The camp had offered accommodation to at least two legions since 14 AD at the latest.[2] Supplying more than 10,000 soldiers on the then sparsely populated Lower Rhine represented a huge logistical challenge that could only be mastered by the creation of a suitable infrastructure (roads, harbour) and the settlement of traders and craftsmen.

After Agrippa had connected the Rhineland to the Roman highway network with the new road from Lyon to Cologne via Trier, the following decades saw the further development of the *viae publicae* in the territory of what was to become the province of Lower Germany. These included the Limes Road, which ran alongside the Rhine. Access to the hinterland included a road that led from Xanten via Heerlen to Cologne.[3] The transport of particularly heavy goods, such as timber and stones, as well as food such as grain and olive oil, was conducted as far as possible by water. A suitable river port was essential for this. Well preserved remains of a harbour quay have been excavated on the east side of the CUT in front of the city wall, opposite insula 36. Drillings for geological investigations prove that the harbour was on the main course of the Rhine and not – as previously suspected – on a side channel. The oldest archaeologically established harbour quay dates back to 46 AD. Dendrochronological analysis shows that reconstruction became necessary in 92 AD and then again forty-five years later (fig. 1). It is still unclear whether the military and civilian population shared the port or whether the military had its own port further upstream.[4] Due to massive post-Roman changes to the course of the Rhine, any harbour for the legionary camp, which may have existed, has been destroyed.

On the Rhine, transport vessels consisted mainly of flat-bottomed boats (barges). The 5–35 m long barge type Zwammerdam is characterized by a large load capacity and a very low draft, so that it was also possible to use it near the shore or at low tide. Evidence for this in the Xanten area are two wrecks as well as other finds of individual parts.[5] The barge from Xanten-Wardt may have been used as a ferry to cross the Rhine.[6] Ceramics and building materials were transported on barges as well as food in sacks, barrels or amphorae. The

Fig. 1: The harbour of the *Colonia Ulpia Traiana*. Virtual reconstruction.

legionnaires stationed in Vetera had manufactured tiles since the 40s of the first century AD. Their products not only covered military needs, but were also used to some extent for public buildings of the CUT.[7] For the construction of the city wall built in the early 2nd century, tuff, which was broken by military detachments in the mines of the volcanic Eifel, had to be shipped first over smaller streams and then along the Rhine to Xanten.[8] Most of the timber procured from the Odenwald and the Black Forest, which was required for pile gratings to create stable foundations or for the casing of foundations in concrete, was most likely brought on barge type Zwammerdam to Xanten.

Archaeological finds of other goods of long-distance and regional trade, which may have reached Xanten mainly by water, include ceramic products of all kinds, especially tableware and kitchenware, and indirectly also those foods that were filled in amphorae such as olive oil and fish sauce from southern Spain, wine from Italy and later from Gaul. Fine tableware was imported from Italy in the early years, then from southern Gaul in the third decade of the first century AD, after production shifted there, to shorten the transport routes to the military sites in the Rhineland.[9] A certain number of goods were also imported from the eastern Mediterranean. These probably included dates, as shown by fragments of Levantine amphorae from the CUT,[10] and various types of marble, which were obtained in the form of sawn plates and used to furnish public buildings.[11]

The needs of the military – and very soon of the growing civilian population – for various craft products, probably led to the establishment of many businesses in the early days of the pre-colonial settlement, and to the emergence of a larger civilian settlement.

Potteries produced a wide range of fine and heavy vessels as well as oil lamps in the area of the later Harbour Temple and at the harbour. Despite the sometimes outstanding quality of the products, they did not find any significant distribution beyond Xanten and the nearby region.[12] The evidence for other craft branches in the pre-colonial settlement and the CUT include workshops for metalworking (coarse and fine smithy), bone carving, tanning or fulling, leather processing, glue boiling, painting and perhaps also brewing. Meat processing workshops (butchery, smokehouse) also seem to have had some importance.[13]

The Batavian revolt in 69/70 AD affected the pre-colony settlement and its further development in ways that are difficult to estimate (Schmitz 2008, 134 note 521). After the end of the revolt, only one legion was stationed in the newly established legionary camp Vetera II. The number of potential buyers of goods and services in the pre-colonial settlement was thus significantly lower than in previous decades. That the settlement was still of (strategic) importance was impressively underlined by the fact that it was raised to the status of a *colonia* in 100 AD.

However, a first inspection of the findings on the craft activities, some of which were published only in preliminary reports, reveals that the majority of these – as far as they are dated – belonged to the pre-colonial settlement. This finding is surprising and needs further investigation. It cannot be ruled out that the special conditions of conservation in the CUT could give a distorted picture – the massive plundering of stones in the Middle Ages and the modern era could disproportionately affect the younger strata. Only after a careful reworking and a more precise dating of the individual findings will we know whether we can assume that there was a decreasing number of craft enterprises in the course of the second and third centuries AD.

Little is known about the direct surroundings of the CUT. So far, only individual findings in the immediate vicinity of the city have been excavated.[14] There is little doubt that the CUT functioned as a central marketplace in the *Civitas Cugernorum*. Here, on market days, the surplus of agricultural production in rural areas was traded, and here the farms of the surrounding area were able to acquire important products such as kitchen utensils, tools and more. This intensive exchange is testified by the high proportion of Roman ceramics in the total ceramics of the indigenous settlements.[15]

Notes

[1] Abstract of my paper presented at the AIAC conference, Bonn 2018. References have been strongly limited, mainly to those contributions published in the last decade.

[2] Hanel 2008.

[3] Andrikopoulou – Jenter 2018.

[4] Selke – Leih 2018.

[5] Obladen-Kauder 2008. 2016.

[6] Schmidhuber-Aspöck 2018.
[7] Schmidts 2018.
[8] Schaaff 2018.
[9] Rudnick 2018.
[10] Höpken 2018.
[11] Ruppiene 2018.
[12] Liesen 2018.
[13] Reuter 2008; Rothenhöfer 2018.
[14] Bridger – Kraus 2008; Bridger 2009.
[15] See the article by M. Brüggler and others in this volume.

Image Credits

Fig. 1: LVR-Archäologischer Park Xanten (virtual reconstruction: Faber-Courtial GbR, Darmstadt).

References

Andrikopoulou – Jenter 2018
N. Andrikopoulou – S. Jenter 2018, Straßen und Verkehr in der Germania Inferior, in: Eger 2018, 201–219.
Bridger – Kraus 2008
C. Bridger – K. Kraus, Die römische Besiedlung der Xantener Bucht, in: Müller et al. 2008, 595–606.
Bridger 2009
C. Bridger, Ausgrabungen entlang der Xantener Umgehungsstraße 2004–2008. 1. Die siedlungsarchäologischen Befunde, in: M. Müller (ed.), Xantener Berichte 15 (Mainz 2009) 235–277.
Eger 2018
Ch. Eger (ed.), Warenwege – Warenflüsse. Handel, Logistik und Transport am römischen Niederrhein. Xantener Berichte 32 (Mainz 2018).
Hanel 2008
N. Hanel, Die Militärlager von Vetera I und ihre Lagersiedlungen, in: Müller et al. 2008, 93–107.
Höpken 2018
C. Höpken, Mediterrane Köstlichkeiten für Xanten – Zu den Amphorenfunden am Niederrhein, in: Eger 2018, 373–387.
Liesen 2018
B. Liesen, Der Handel mit Keramik aus Niedergermanien und angrenzenden Gebieten, in: Eger 2018, 361–372.
Müller et al. 2008
M. Müller – H.-J. Schalles – N. Zieling (eds.), Colonia Ulpia Traiana. Xanten und sein Umland in römischer Zeit, Xantener Berichte Sonderband (Mainz 2008).

Obladen-Kauder 2008
J. Obladen-Kauder, Spuren römischer Lastschifffahrt am unteren Niederrhein, in: Müller et al. 2008, 507–523.

Obladen-Kauder 2016
J. Obladen-Kauder, Wieder einmal Teile eines Schiffes aus einer Xantener Kiesgrube, in: J. Kunow – M. Trier (eds.), Archäologie im Rheinland 2015 (Darmstadt 2016) 117–118.

Reuter 2008
M. Reuter, Wirtschaftsstandort Colonia Ulpia Traiana – Handel und Handwerk in der CUT, in: Müller et al. 2008, 471–493.

Rothenhöfer 2018
P. Rothenhöfer, Wirtschaft und Handel am unteren Niederrhein, in: Eger 2018, 69–88.

Rudnick 2018
B. Rudnick, First to the Market – Zur Marktorientierung römischer Qualitätsgeschirr-produzenten aus Italien und Südgallien, in: Eger 2018, 339–360.

Ruppiene 2018
V. Ruppiene, Marmora in der CUT und ihr Weg an den Niederrhein, in: Eger 2018, 407–422.

Schaaff 2018
H. Schaaff, Steine, Städte und Soldaten – Zu den staatlichen bauprogrammen in der Germania Inferior, in: Eger 2018, 157–176.

Schmidhuber-Aspöck 2018
G. Schmidhuber-Aspöck, Binnenschifffahrt auf dem Rhein in römischer Zeit in: Eger 2018, 229–243.

Schmidts 2018
Th. Schmidts, Die Legionsziegeleien – Römische Baustoffindustrie am Niederrhein, in: Eger 2018, 133–155.

Schmitz 2008
D. Schmitz, Der Bataveraufstand im Kontext des römischen Bürgerkrieges 68–70 n. Chr., in: Müller et al. 2008, 117–140.

Selke – Leih 2018
V. Selke – S. Leih, Der Hafen der Colonia Ulpia Traiana, in: Eger 2018, 271–288.

The Hinterland of the *Colonia Ulpia Traiana* (Xanten): Supply Basis for the Town?

Marion Brüggler – Renate Gerlach – Jutta Meurers-Balke – Tanja Zerl – Michael Herchenbach

The territory of the *Colonia Ulpia Traiana* comprised two *civitates*: the *civitas* of the *Cugerni* in the north and the *civitas* of the *Baetasii* in the south (fig. 1). Their landscapes were very different: While the *Baetasii* lived in the loess-belt with its high quality soils, the *Cugerni* inhabited a landscape of loamy and sandy soils with small scale changes of soil-types. This natural divide is virtually identical with the delimination of the distribution of *villae rusticae* and divides the Rhineland into a southern "villa landscape" and a northern "non-villa landscape". The border between the two lies a little to the north of the modern towns of Mönchengladbach and Neuss.[1]

In this paper, we will focus more on the northern part of the territory of the *Colonia Ulpia Traiana*, i.e. the immediate hinterland of the colony. The archaeological record here is still rather sparse, compared to other parts of the province *Germania inferior*.[2] Only in the last decade sites with Roman-period farms were excavated; accordingly, only a handful is known so far. Concerning our question whether the hinterland was a supply basis for the town, we can refer to settlement layouts, the material culture found in these settlements and archaeobotanical data. Unfortunately, no zooarchaeological data is available due to lack of preservation of bones in these soils.

Excavated settlements show byre-houses constructed of non-permanent materials. At the site Weeze-Vorselaer (fig. 2) the earliest buildings of the Roman period can be dated to Augustan times. These early byre-houses were still relatively small with lengths under 20 m. The younger houses of the site belonging to the 2nd and 3rd centuries and those from the sites Kevelaer-Grotendonk and Wachtendonk-Meerendonkshof were considerably larger with lengths up to 30 m. These settlements consisted of single farms. As the byre-part of the houses demonstrates, cattle seemed to have played an economic role.[3]

The density of settlement and thus also the availability of labour to grow crops and raise cattle is of course important for our question of supplying the town. Counting only the few excavated sites, we would have to negate the possibility. For a better understanding of settlement density, therefore, surface finds and reports of finds made in the 19th and the first half of the 20th century, which are kept in the database of the LVR-State Service for Archaeological Heritage in the Rhineland, have to be drawn upon as settlement indicators. The picture is that of a well settled region, though with gaps and concentrations of findspots (fig. 3). Settlement sites lie on low elevations (so-called Donken) in the Niers-plain – the river Niers being a tributary of the river Meuse – and on the southwestern slopes of the push moraines, which were formed during the Saale-Glaciation. Areas with wet soils and bogs are not settled. Clusters of findspots are located especially on the heights of the Reichswald push moraine. These are likely the result of

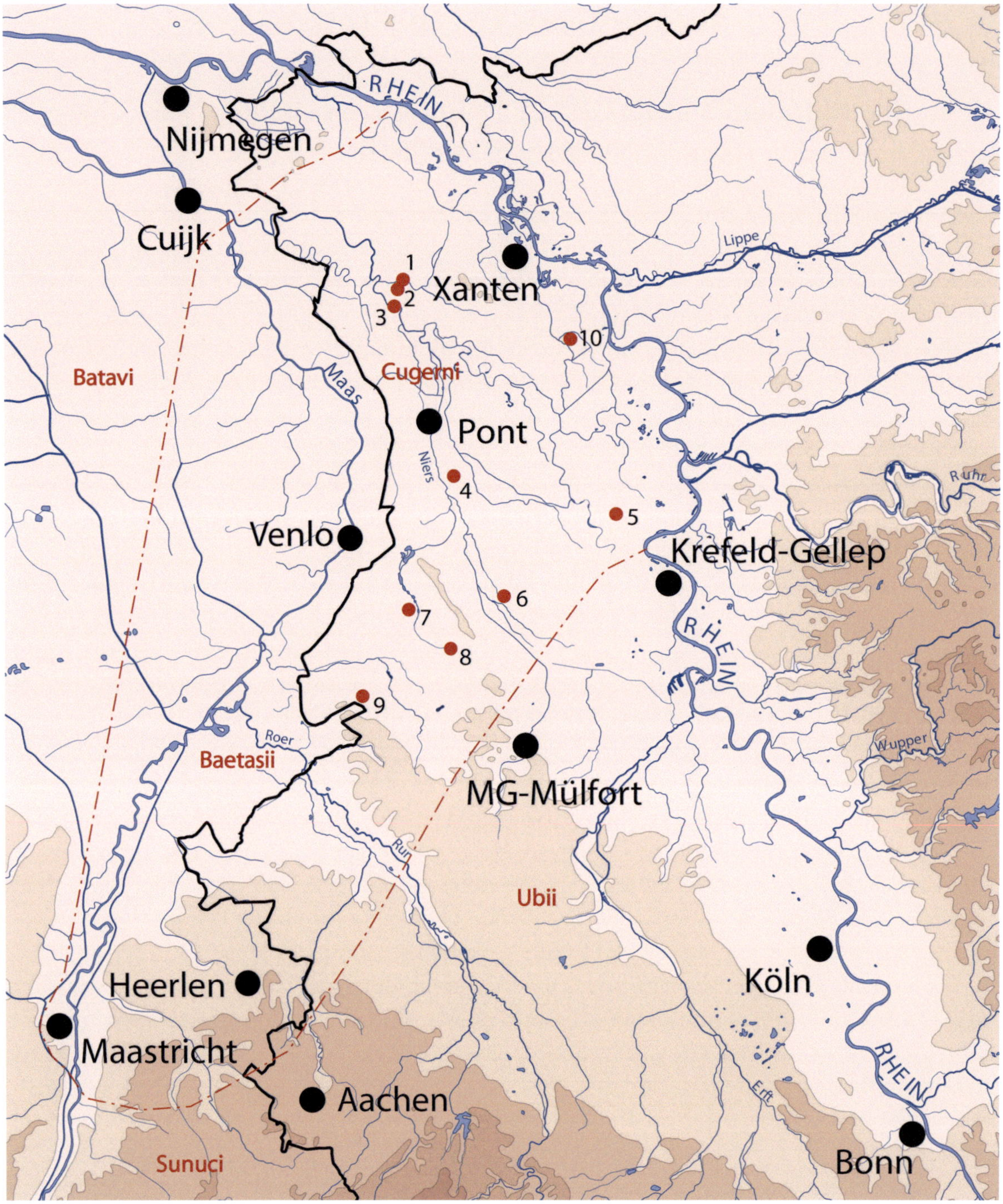

Fig. 1: Territory of the *Colonia Ulpia Traiana*. Numbers: (partially) excavated agricultural sites: 1) Kevelaer-Grotendonk, 2) Weeze-Vorselaer, 3) Weeze-Seisterather Hof, 4) Wachtendonk-Meerendonkshof, 5) Krefeld-Vennikel, 6) Tönisvorst, 7) Nettetal-Breyell, 8) Viersen-Dülken, 9) Niederkrüchten-Boschershausen, 10) Alpen.

Fig. 2: Plan of the site Weeze-Vorselaer.

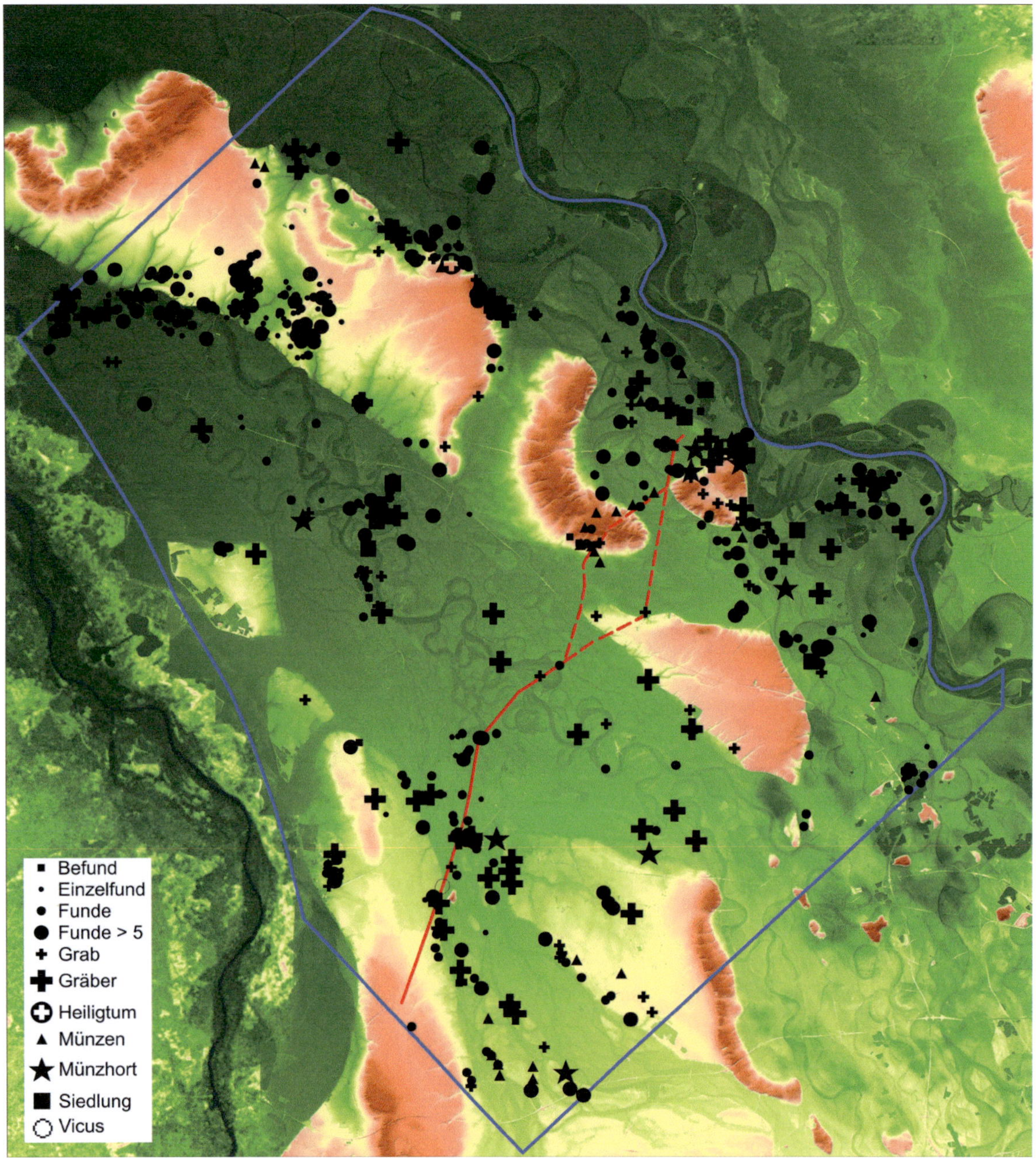

Fig. 3: Potential Roman settlement sites. Data to the east of the Rhine has not been mapped. Elevations are between 15 (green) and 100 m (brown) above sealevel.

research intensity,[4] but may well give an indication of actual site concentrations. On the floodplain of the river Rhine, the meandering of the river has completely reworked large areas in post Roman times, so an evaluation of Roman settlement here is difficult. Along the Limes-road military sites such as forts, watchtowers and numerous training camps

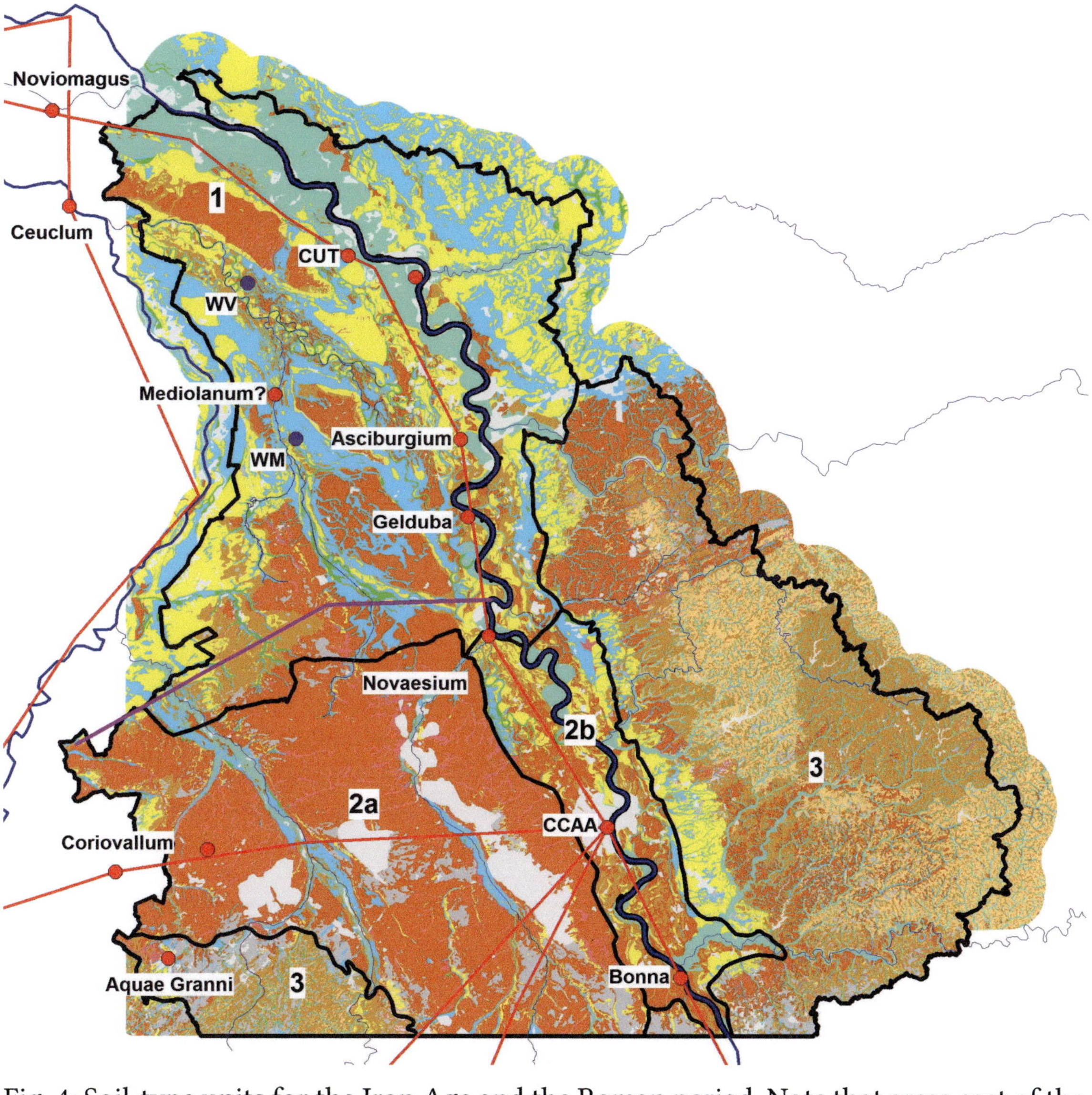

Fig. 4: Soil-type units for the Iron Age and the Roman period. Note that areas east of the River Rhine have been mapped, but not included into the calculation.

dominate the picture. Apart from an area to the southeast of the *Colonia Ulpia Traiana*, deliminated by a large meander of the river Rhine, there are no certain indications of civilian, agricultural settlements in the Limes-road.

Since the dataset allows only a general picture and is heavily biased due to the state of research, we have tried to reason the other way round: we checked the availability of land usable for farming. The digital soil-map of the „Geologische Dienst" of North Rhine-Westfalia (State Geological Service) was evaluated in this respect. We have analysed the distribution of soil-types (fig. 4) and classified them into soil-value classes (fig. 5). Though the map is based on the modern soil-map, it is not identical. Certain models have been used to establish a plausible model regarding soil-conditions in Antiquity.[5]

Luvisols possess a high to very high agricultural potential and are therefore used as arable land. They are suitable for the cultivation of demanding crops such as bread wheat (*Triticum aestivum*) and spelt (*Triticum spelta*) and are therefore categorised into the "high" and "very high" soil value classes. These soils make up 25% of the area on the lower Rhine compared to 55% in the loess-area. Cambisols on loamy parent material cover 12% of the northern area compared to 6% in the loess-landscape. They have a high agricultural potential, although not as high as the Luvisols on loess. Even so, these soils are suitable for cultivating demanding cereals. 22% of the soils in the northern area are Podsols and Cambisols on sandy parent material, compared to 5% in the southern area. The latter have middle to low soil values. Arable farming is possible on the more loamy-sandy soils (middle), especially if less demanding crops like barley (*Hordeum vulgare*) and millet (*Panicum miliaceum/Setaria italic*) are cultivated. Gleysols, Histosols and Stagnosols, for which soil wetness is characteristic, comprise 26% of the northern area and only 11% in the southern area. The wet root-zone in these soils reduces their potential for arable farming; they therefore have only limited productivity and are used as meadows and pastures. The Fluvisols of the Rhine floodplain are generally nutrient-rich – because they are regularly fertilised by floods – and therefore possess high agricultural potential. 11% of the northern region are covered by these soils and 4% of the southern region. The constant danger of flooding, however, was a limiting factor before the construction of the dykes along the river Rhine, which started in the 13th century. These soils could therefore rather be used as meadows and pastures and not for crop cultivation.

The main differences between the two natural units are soil properties and quality. While the southern Rhineland to the west of the river Rhine is dominated by a closed loess layer with very good soil properties, the Lower Rhine Plain in the northern lowlands exhibits more diversity. There is a small-scale alternation between different soil-types and in total the values of the different soil-types were less suitable for a more demanding cereal-based agriculture. Even though this landscape is less fertile than the loess-region, the soils in the hinterland of the *Colonia Ulpia Traiana* cannot be called infertile and poor, the potential was there. As a simplification, one can speak of a loess landscape and a less-loess landscape, because there are some loess islands also in the northern part.

To sum up: in the northern region, 70% of the land can be used for agriculture with 27% having „spelt quality" and 42% "barley quality". 27% are usable as meadows and pastures. The southern region has 83% arable land, with 68% of "spelt quality", 15% "barley quality" and 7% usable only for meadows and pastures.

	Lower Rhine Plain (I) 2705 km²		suitable for		
Soil value classes (GD NRW)	km²	%	demanding cereals	less demanding crops	livestock
very high	23,50	0,87	+	+	+
high	716,10	26,47	+	+	+
middle (incl. Fluvisols)	1437,60	53,15		+	+
low and very low	442,10	16,34			+
Disturbances	85,10	3,15			
Total:	2705,00	100,00	-	-	-

	Cologne Bay (II) 3060 km²		suitable for		
Soil value classes (GD NRW)	km²	%	demanding cereals	less demanding crops	livestock
very high	1185,00	38,73	+	+	+
high	890,58	29,10	+	+	+
middle (incl. Fluvisols)	587,52	19,20		+	+
low and very low	77,35	2,53			+
Disturbances	319,70	10,45			
Total:	3060,00	100,00	-	-	-

In the last paragraphs, we considered the potential of the soils in the Roman period. But what kind of vegetation actually grew there? Here, we can refer to the pollen diagram from Kleefsche Beek (fig. 6).[6] It encompasses the period from the Neolithic to the Early Modern period. This diagram comes from a site located on the floodplain of the river Meuse near Gennep (NL) and can be taken as representing the vegetation history of the whole of the Lower Rhine-Meuse region. The Iron Age pollen spectrum already reveals a high proportion of herbaceous plants and grasses. We have to surmise that vast woodland no longer existed by the Iron Age,[7] rather, some copses, groups of trees and bushes were scattered among the fields and pastures. Pollen proportions of 20–40% of herbaceous plants point to a largely open, cultivated landscape, a development that had started in the late Bronze Age. Development of heather as an indicator of overexploitation can already be seen at the start of the Iron Age. Obviously, with the Iron Age, animal husbandry had

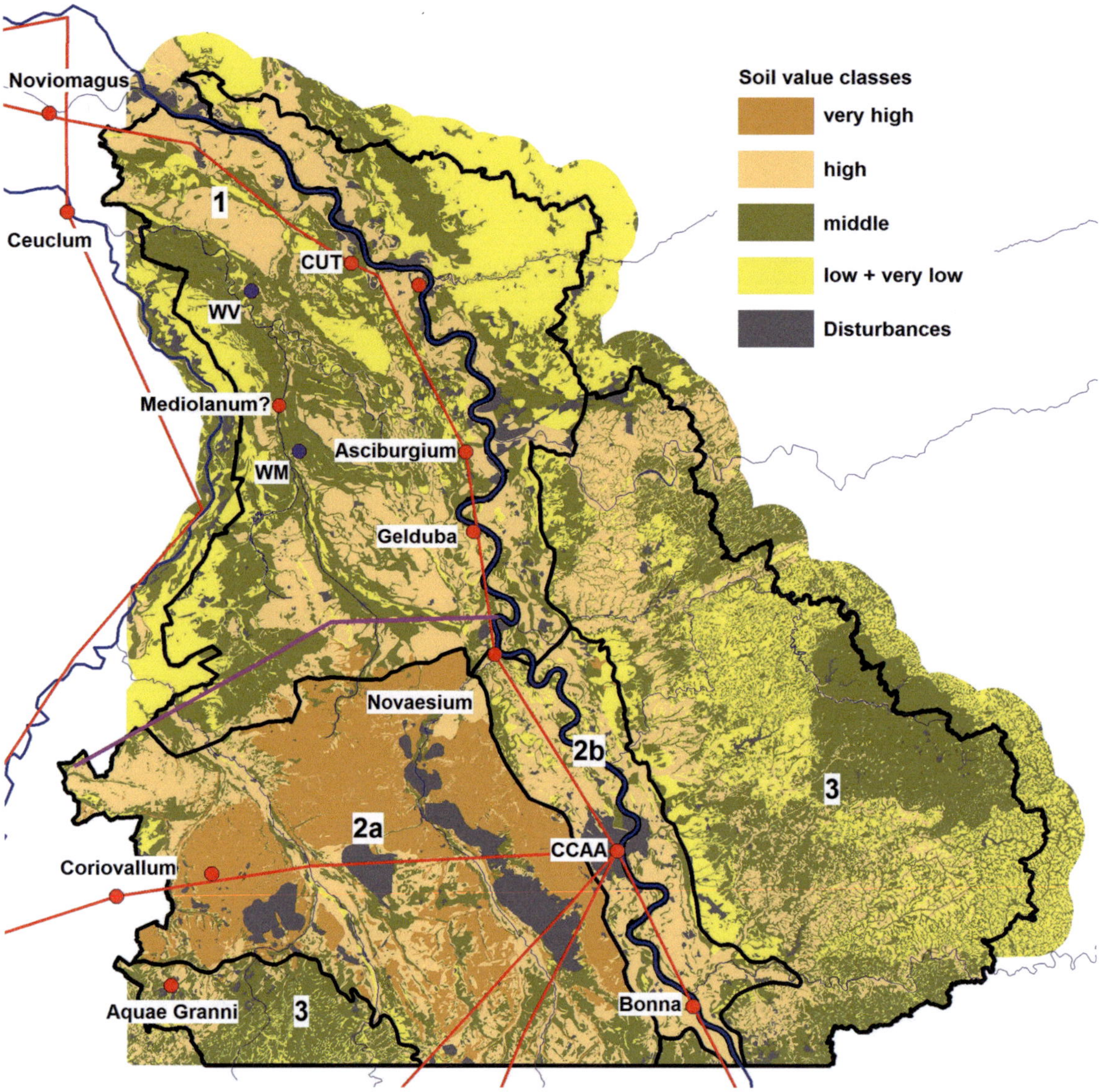

Fig. 5: Soil value classes.

changed significantly. It was no longer predominantly based on wood pasture and leaf-foddering, but on grazing on meadows. This led to the development of grass vegetation and – on nutrient-poor sandy soils – to the development of heathland. At the same time the area used for arable farming was probably expanded; this can be seen by the rise in cereal pollen in the diagram. Less woodland already in the Iron Age means less retention capability with the rise of the ground water level and as a result more wet soils and spreading of gleysols.[8] Furthermore, wet areas with alder forests get cleared. There seems to be pressure on the land, otherwise these low quality lands would not have been used.

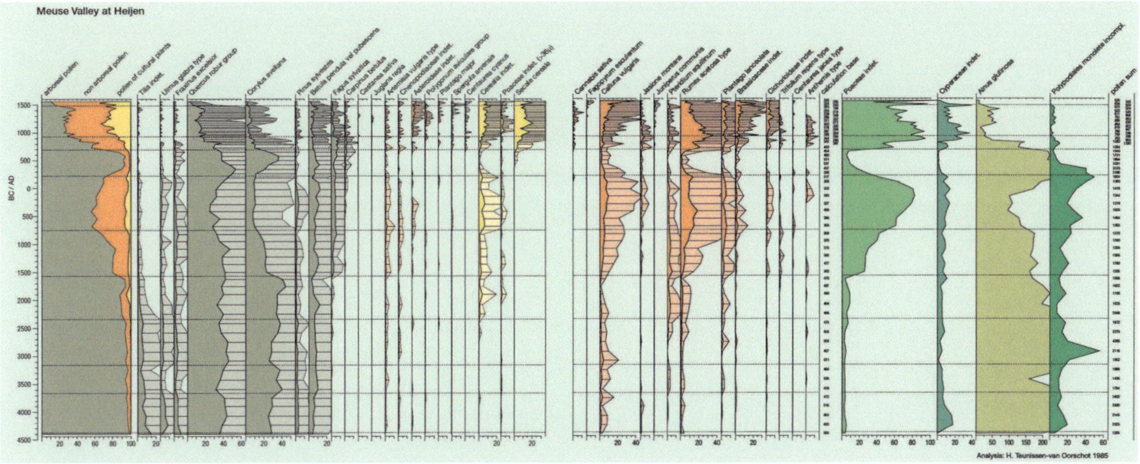

Fig. 6: Pollendiagram Kleefsche Beek.

Pollen indicating agriculture and also heather recede in Roman times. This is, however, not a result of population decline. In the opposite: Population density seems to increase and, at least in the southern parts of the Rhineland, a surplus in production is reached. How do these findings fit? It is a result of marginal soils being taken out of use and the regrowth of riverside forests. In the northern region, agriculture is still practised in Iron Age tradition, but it seems to be more efficient now. So, the farmers must have made something different than before. There might have been innovations, which we are unable to grasp at the moment. One explanation might be a decrease of sheep- and goat-husbandry in favour of cattle and horse, now on the higher quality soils.

Could the population of the CUT-hinterland IN THEORY supply the town (and the closest forts at the Limes)? The same question had been asked by Laura Kooistra, Marieke van Dinter and others for the Rhine estuary and answered through a model calculation.[9] Their assumptions were adapted for our working area (roughly the area between Nijmegen and Gellep).[10] We have looked at cereals and cattle demand on the one hand and possible production on the other hand. We had to estimate the inhabitants of the towns and forts, and also of the hinterland and their daily demand in cereals and cattle. According to this calculation, the rural population should have been able to create a surplus in cereal to supply the town. As we have shown above, the limiting factor was obviously not the land availability. Enough land was available for growing cereals, even demanding cereals such as spelt. Concerning cattle, land for meadows pastures was abundant. However, the number of farms seems – according to our knowledge of the settlement density and the assumptions underlying this model – not to have been high enough to create a surplus in cattle.

Which crops were grown in the hinterland of the *Colonia Ulpia Traiana*? Recently, the Weeze-Vorselaer and Wachtendonk-Meerendonkshof sites have provided new archaeobotanical evidence (fig. 7). Both settlements exhibit a spectrum of cultivated plants

	CCAA	CUT	settlements, loess (villae)	settlements, non loess
Cereals				
spelt (*Triticum spelta*)	⬤	⬤	⬤	·
emmer (*Triticum dicoccon*)	●	●	●	•
barley (*Hordeum vulgare*)	•	●	●	⬤
millet (*Panicum miliaceum/Setaria italica*)	•	○	○	●
free-threshing wheat (*Triticum aestivum* vel *durum*)	○	○	○	
einkorn (*Triticum monococcum*)	·	·	·	·
Pulses				
lentil (*Lens culinaris*)	·	○	·	·
pea (*Pisum sativum*)	·	·	·	
celtic bean (*Vicia faba*)	·	○		(+)
common vetch (*Vicia sativa*)	·	+	·	
bitter vetch (*Vicia ervilia*)			·	·
flax (*Linum usitatissimum*)	•	•	·	+
poppy (*Papaver somniferum*)	•	•	·	
gold-of-pleasure (*Camelina sativa*)	·	·	·	
dill (*Anethum graveolens*)	•	•	·	
celery (*Apium graveolens*)	•	•	·	
coriander (*Coriandrum satvum*)	•	•	·	
summer savory (*Satureja hortensis*)	•	•	·	
fennel (*Foeniculum vulgare*)	·	·	+	
anise (*Pimpinella anisum*)	(+)	·	·	
rue (*Ruta graveolens*)	+	+		
cumin (*Cuminum cyminum*)	+	(+)		
Fruits				
sweet cherry (*Prunus avium*)	●	●	•	+
apple (*Malus domestica*)	●	●	·	
pear (*Pyrus communis*)	●	●	·	
cultivated vine (*Vitis vinifera*)	●	●	·	
walnut (*Juglans regia*)	•	•	·	
bullace plum (*Prunus insititia*)	•	•	(+)	
plum (*Prunus domestica*)	·	·	+	
peach (*Prunus persica*)	·	·	+	
cornelian cherry (*Cornus mas*)	·	+	+	
black mulberry (*Morus nigra*)	·	+	+	
cucumber (*Cucumis sativus*)	·	+		
medlar (*Mespilus germanica*)	·	(+)		
sorb apple (*Sorbus domestica*)		+		
Import				
fig (*Ficus carica*)	●	●	·	
date (*Phoenix dactylifera*)	○	·		
pomegranate (*Punica granatum*)	·	+		
caper (*Capparis spinosa*)	+	·		
pepper (*Piper nigrum*)	+	+		
olive (*Olea europaea*)	+	+		
stone pine (*Pinus pinea*)	+	+		

⬤ dominant
● frequent in larger quantities
• frequent in small quantities
○ sporadic in larger quantities
· sporadic
\+ single find
(+) uncertain

Fig. 7: Crop plants in the *Colonia Claudia Ara Agrippinensium* (CCAA), the *Colonia Ulpia Traiana* (CUT), in rural settlements in the Cologne bay (loess) and the Lower Rhine Plain (less-loess).

that very much resembles that of Iron Age sites: barley (*Hordeum vulgare*) predominates, broomcorn and foxtail millet (*Panicum miliaceum, Setaria italica*) were also important; emmer (*Triticum dicoccon*) and sporadically spelt (*Triticum spelta*) have been found. A few pulses occur, such as lentil (*Lens culinaris*), bitter vetch (*Vicia ervilia*) and probably also celtic bean (*Vicia faba*); flax (*Linum usitatissimum*), too, is found. Likewise, the weed flora correlates to that of the Iron Age; taxa typical for Roman farming on the loess are absent. This is true for the cultivated crops as well. There are no indications of vegetables, spices and cultivated fruit, apart from two stones of sweet cherry (*Prunus avium*) from a well in Wachtendonk-Meerendonkshof.[11] Although they lived close to the Roman town, the farmers of the hinterland kept to a traditional (Iron Age) food pattern. If we compare the kinds of crops grown in the hinterland and consumed in the towns, the following picture emerges. The provincial capital *Colonia Claudia Ara Agrippinensium* (CCAA) and the *Colonia Ulpia Traiana* (CUT) are alike in their consumption pattern. The same pattern is evident in the loess-area, i.e. the hinterland of the CCAA, but the hinterland of the CUT differs. According to this evidence, it is obvious that the immediate hinterland did not grow cereals like spelt for provisioning the CUT. Furthermore, charred spelt-massfinds from the CUT contain typical weeds from calcareous soils, which cannot be found in the hinterland of the CUT.[12] The grain therefore has been brought in from suitable soils.

To sum up: Spelt is the dominant bread crop in Roman towns and forts on the Lower Rhine. Its cultivation in the Rhineland takes place in the villa-system in the loess-landscape, where people built, cultivated and consumed in Roman style. There is enough land of sufficient quality available also on the lower Rhine to cultivate crops and supply for the CUT, but spelt is not cultivated on a larger scale and the villa-system is not introduced here. A possible reason is that the small scale change of soils against the uniformity of the soil in the south did not allow the same use of more efficient farming techniques. Other reasons for not introducing a villa-system could also have been different structures of societies.

Even though obviously no fruit, no herbs, no spelt for the CUT were cultivated in its hinterland, some kind of economic interaction must have taken place, as the occurrence of Roman-made pottery in the vernacular farmsteads shows. The local population must have acquired it – and certainly other goods we are unable to grasp archaeologically. The growth of the farm buildings and an increase in the number of settlements during middle Roman period even indicate economic growth. So, what was the basis for this exchange?

Animal husbandry is often cited for the landscapes of the Lower Rhine,[13] only: no bones survived in the hinterland due to the sandy soils so no direct comparison can be made. According to the model explained above, the surplus in cattle would not be high enough. Of course, the model may be wrong (there were more producers and less consumption than surmised for the model calculation).

Research into the hinterland of the *Colonia Ulpia Traiana* is still at the beginning, compared to the neighbouring regions to the west of the Meuse, where development led-archaeology has resulted in the excavation and publication of many more agricultural settlements of the Roman era. The evaluation of the recent excavations and comparison with other, better researched areas in *Germania inferior*, are promising further insights into economic and social developments, which will lead to a better understanding of town-country relations of the *Colonia Ulpia Traiana*. Concerning the immediate question of the provenience of cattle, isotopic analysis of cattle-bones from the *Colonia Ulpia Traiana*, where there were better preservation conditions than in the hinterland, might help to establish knowledge on trade networks for this commodity.

Notes

[1] Heimberg 2002/2003; Cott 2017.

[2] cf. Jeneson 2017, 31–40.

[3] cf. Brüggler 2017, 40–53 for a more detailed description of the sites and Langenhoff 2018 for an evaluation of the Wachtendonk-site.

[4] The area to the east of the confluence of Niers and Meuse was researched by Riedmeier-Fischer (1998) and an amateur-archaeologist, who conducted intensive and systematic field walking.

[5] cf. Gerlach et al. 2017, 73 f. for a more detailed description.

[6] Kalis et al. 2008; cf. also Gerlach et al. 2017, 80–86.

[7] The apparent predominance of arboreal pollen in the diagram is due to the fact that this derives from wind-pollinating trees and shrubs which have high pollen productivity and pollen which is dispersed by wind across a wide area.

[8] Gerlach – Meurers-Balke 2015.

[9] Kooistra et al. 2013; van Dinter et al. 2014.

[10] cf. Brüggler et al. 2017, 65–70 for details on the calculation.

[11] Gerlach et al. 2017, 82.

[12] Herchenbach – Meurers-Balke – Zerl in prep.

[13] Nolde (2018) implies that cattle was produced locally. Cf. also Roymans et al. 2015 for the neighbouring Meuse-Demer-Schelde area.

Image Credits

Fig. 1: Territorial borders after Bridger 2008. Map: Chr. Duntze, LVR-Landesmuseum Bonn. Layout: M. Brüggler, LVR-Amt für Bodendenkmalpflege im Rheinland. – Fig. 2: Layout: M. Brüggler, LVR-Amt für Bodendenkmalpflege im Rheinland. – Fig. 3: M. Brüggler, LVR-Amt für Bodendenkmalpflege im Rheinland, on the basis of DGM25, © Geobasis NRW. – Fig. 4–5: R. Lubberich, LVR-Amt für Bodendenkmalpflege im Rheinland, on the basis of Bodenübersichtskarte 1:50,000 Geologischer Dienst NRW. – Fig. 6: Kalis et al. 2008, analysis H. Teunissen-van Oorschot 1985. – Fig. 7: T. Zerl, Labor für Archäobotanik, University of Cologne.

References

Bridger 2008
C. Brigder, Die civitas Traianensis - das römische Umland von Xanten, in: M. Müller – H.-J. Schalles – N. Zieling (eds.), Colonia Ulpia Traiana. Xanten und sein Umland in römischer Zeit. Xantener Berichte Sonderband (Mainz 2008) 607–626.

Brüggler et al. 2017
M. Brüggler – K. Jeneson – R. Gerlach – J. Meurers-Balke – T. Zerl – M. Herchenbach, The Roman Rhineland. Farming and Consumption in Different Landscapes, in: M. Reddé (ed.), Gallia Rustica 1. Les Campagnes du Nord-Est de la Gaule, de la Fin de l'Âge du Fer à l'Antiquité Tardive (Bordeaux 2017) 19–95.

Cott 2017
E. Cott, Die Übergangsregion zwischen Erkelenz und Nettetal – römische Fundstellen und ihr landschaftlicher Kontext, in: J. Kunow – M. Trier (eds.), Archäologie im Rheinland 2016 (Darmstadt 2017) 121–123.

Gerlach – Meurers-Balke 2015
R. Gerlach – J. Meurers-Balke, Neolithische Landschaften im Rheinland und Westfalen, in: T. Otten – J. Kunow – M. Rind – M. Trier (eds.), Archäologie in NRW 2010–2015. Revolution jungSteinzeit. Archäologische Landesausstellung Nordrhein-Westfalen. Schriften zur Bodendenkmalpflege in Nordrhein-Westfalen 11.1 (Darmstadt 2015) 171–177.

Heimberg 2002
U. Heimberg, Römische Villen an Rhein und Maas, BJb 202, 2002, 57–148.

Herchenbach – Meurers-Balke – Zerl in prep.
Archäobotanik in Xanten (provisional title). Xantener Berichte NN.

Kalis et al. 2008
A.J. Kalis – S. Karg – J. Meurers-Balke – H. Teunissen-van Oorschot, Mensch und Vegetation am Unteren Niederrhein während der Eisen- und Römerzeit, in: M. Müller – H.-J. Schalles – N. Zieling (eds.), Colonia Ulpia Traiana. Xanten und sein Umland in römischer Zeit. Xantener Berichte Sonderband (Mainz 2008) 31–48.

Kooistra et al. 2013
L.I. Kooistra – M. van Dinter – M.K. Dütting – P. van Rijn – C. Cavallo, Could the Local Population of the Lower Rhine Delta Supply the Roman Army? Part 1: The Archaeological and Historical Framework. Journal of Archaeology in the Low Countries 4, 2013, 5–23.

Langenhoff 2018
Th. Langenhoff, Die römerzeitliche Siedlung bei Wachtendonk-Meerendonkshof, Kreis Kleve (Master-thesis, Freiburg i. Br. 2018).

Nolde 2018
N. Nolde, Mit dem Ochs über den Berg? Zur Frage der Rinderimporte in der Colonia Ulpia Traiana bei Xanten, in: Ch. Eger (ed.), Warenwege – Warenflüsse. Handel, Logistik und Transport am römischen Niederrhein, Xantener Berichte 32 (Mainz 2018) 443–450.

Riedmeier-Fischer 1998
E. Riedmeier-Fischer, Siedlungsarchäologische Untersuchungen im Raum zwischen Niers und Kendel, BJb 198, 1998, 129–283.

Roymans et al. 2015
N. Roymans – T. Derks – H. Hiddink (eds.), The Roman Villa of Hoogeloon and the Archaeology of the Periphery. Amsterdam Archaeological Studies 22 (Amsterdam 2015).

van Dinter et al. 2014
M. van Dinter – L.I. Kooistra – M.K. Dütting – P. van Rijn, C. Cavallo, Could the Local Population of the Lower Rhine Delta Supply the Roman Army? Part 2: Modelling the Carrying Capacity Using Archaeological, Palaeo-ecological and Geomorphological Data, Journal of Archaeology in the Low Countries 5, 2014, 5–50.

Printing and Binding
Books on Demand GmbH, Norderstedt